ART AND HISTORY
OF
ROME

215 COLOR PICTURES

BONECHI

© Copyright 1997 by
CASA EDITRICE BONECHI -
Via Cairoli, 18/b
50131 FIRENZE - ITALIA
Telex 571323 CEB
Fax 55-5000766
Tel. 55-576841

Printed in Italy by
Centro Stampa Editoriale Bonechi.

Text by: Fabio Boldrini, Leonardo Castellucci, Stefano
Giuntoli, Riccardo Mazzanti and Giulia Menotti.

Translation by: Erika Pauli, for Studio COMUNICARE, Florence.

*The photographs are the property of the Archives of Casa
Editrice Bonechi and were taken by:*
Gaetano Barone, Gianni Dagli Orti, Paolo Giambone, Grifoni,
Maurilio Mazzola, Mario Tonini.
*The photographs of the restored frescoes of the Sistine Chapel
are a courtesy of:* Foto Musei Vaticani, pages 101 bottom, 104,
108-112; NTV Tokyo, pages 105-107, 113-114.

ISBN 88-8029-115-7

INTRODUCTION

HISTORY

Rome began when groups of shepherds and farmers settled on the hill now known as the Palatine. Etymologically Roma *may mean the city of the river, or more probably the city of the Ruma, an old Etruscan family.*
After the semi-legendary period of the monarchy, the first authentic historical references date to the moment of transition from the monarchy to the republic (509 B.C.), when the Etruscan civilization, which had dominated Rome with the last kings, began its slow decline. The long period of the republic was marked by the formation of a real democracy governed by the consuls and the tribunes (the latter represented the so-called plebeians), which went so far as to institute equal rights for patricians and plebs.
In the 4th century B.C. Rome already held sway over all of Latium and later extended its rule to many other regions in Italy, subjugating numerous Italic peoples and the great Etruscan civilization. Even the Gauls, and the Greeks in southern Italy, laid down their arms to Rome and by 270 B.C. the entire Italian peninsula had fallen under Roman domination. In the 3rd century B.C. this power began to spread out beyond the borders of the peninsula. Between 264 and 201 B.C. the entire Mediterranean (with the Punic wars) fell under Roman rule, and in the east, Rome extended its frontiers into Alexander the Great's kingdom, and in the west, subjugated the Gauls and the peoples of Spain. It is at this point that the republic became an empire, beginning with auspices of power and greatness under Augustus.
The empire, as it was conceived, was meant to be a balanced mixture of the various republican magistratures under the direct control of the senate and the will of the people. This was what it was meant to be, but in reality as time passed the empire took on an ever increasing dictatorial and militaristic aspect. With its far-flung frontiers, Rome found itself divided and split and as its authority began to wane, it went into a slow but inexorable decadence. The city was no longer the emperor's seat and the senate continued to lose its political identity. This decadence reached its zenith after the first barbarian invasions, but the city never lost its moral force, that awareness which for centuries had considered Rome the caput mundi, *a situation which was also abetted by the advent of Christianity which consecrated it as the seat of its Church.*
After the middle of the 6th century A.D., Rome became just another of the cities of the new Byzantine empire, with its capital in Ravenna. Even so, two centuries later, thanks to the presence of the Pope, it once more became a reference point for this empire and its history becomes inseparable from that of the Franco-Carolingian empire. Charlemagne chose to be crowned emperor in Rome and hereafter all emperors were to be consecrated as such in Rome.
The city proclaimed itself a free commune in 1144. In this period it was governed by the municipal powers, the papacy and the feudal nobility. The powers of the commune and those of the pope were often in open contrast and were marked by harsh struggles. At the beginning of the 14th century the papacy moved to Avignon and the popular forces were freer to govern. At the end of the 14th century and in the early 15th century the situation once more was reversed: the pope returned to Rome and managed to gain control of the city and recuperate most of the power the popular government had gained in the preceding century. The city flourished in this period, for it became the capital of the Papal State and was as splendid as ever, one of the most important crossroads for culture and art. In the centuries that followed, politically Rome tended towards an ever greater isolation: the Papal State kept at a distance from the various international contrasts and while this set limits on its importance from a political point of view it gave free rein to a development of trade and above all the arts and culture.
This situation continued up to the end of the 18th century when the revolutionary clime which struck Europe in those years also involved the Church in an unexpected crisis and the papal rule of the city passed to the Republic (Pius VI was exiled to France). Temporal power had a brief comeback with Pius VII, but only a few years later Napoleon once more revolutionized the situation, proclaiming Rome the second city of his empire. After varying vicissitudes in which the city returned to the pope (1814), came the period of the Risorgimento when, under the papacy of Pius IX, Rome was a ferment of patriotic and anticlerical ideals. In 1848 a real parliament was formed; the following year the Roman Republic was proclaimed and the government passed into the hands of a triumvirate headed by Giuseppe Mazzini until the intervention of the French army restored temporal power. In 1860 with the formation of the Kingdom of Italy, the pope's power was limited to Latium alone. Ten years later, with the famous episode of the breach at Porta Pia, the French troops protecting the papacy were driven out of the city, which was annexed to the Kingdom of Italy and became its capital. Dissension arose between the Papal State and the new Italian political reality which eventually led to the conciliation between the State and the Church in the Lateran Pact (Feb. 11, 1929). After World War II, when Italy passed from the monarchy to the republic, Rome became the seat of the Italian Parliament.

Mosaic from the 3rd century featuring a charioteer of Circus Maximus. Museo Nazionale delle Terme.

ARCHITECTURE

*I*n the beginning Rome developed on the Palatine hill and gradually spread to the surrounding hills. The Servian walls *date to the 4th century B.C. The circuit of* Aurelian walls *are later. The urban fabric changed almost radically during the felicitous period of the Republic and the city expanded rapidly (the* Cloaca Maxima *and the* Basilica Aemilia *belong to this period). With the advent of the empire, the city expanded still further (marked by the imposing* Imperial Fora, *the* Basilica Julia, *the reliefs on* Trajan's Column *and on that of* Marcus Aurelius, *the reliefs on the* Arch of Titus *and those on the* Arch of Septimius Severus, *the* Pantheon, *the* Colosseum, *Nero's* Domus Aurea *and* Trajan's Markets, *the* Baths of Caracalla *and of* Diocletian).

After the fires of A.D. 64 and 80, Rome was almost completely rebuilt on a more modern and rational plan. In the 2nd century A.D. the population of the city numbered about a million inhabitants, unusual for the times. The city began to decline in the 3rd century and a new circuit of walls went up. The haunting catacombs (brought to light in the 20th century) date to the 3rd and 4th centuries and the magnificent mosaics of S. Pudenziana *and of* SS. Cosma and Damiano *are not much later.*

With the arrival of the Goths and then of the Lombards, Rome was practically deserted (50,000 inhabitants) and the development of the arts came to a standstill. Numerous churches, including those of Santa Maria Maggiore, Santa Sabina *and* San Clemente, *were built in the early Christian period.*

In the 9th century the city was demolished by the Saracens and then in 1084 by the Normans. In the 10th, 11th, and 12th centuries the cultural awakening of the city began (with the Romanesque churches of San Clemente, Santa Maria in Trastevere, San Crisogono). *The Romanesque style was replaced by the Gothic style, which, however, left few signs in the city (*Church of Santa Maria sopra Minerva, *the ciboria* Arnolfo di Cambio *made for the* Churches of San Paolo *and* Santa Cecilia). *Not until the papacy returned to Rome after its period of exile in Avignon did Rome rapidly return to its role of being an exceedingly important crossroads for culture and trade.*

During the 15th century, under the impulse of the Church, the city flourished once more. Many of the most illustrious artists worked for the Vatican. Works of art realized in this period include the bronze doors of St. Peter's *by Filarete; the decoration of the* Vatican Chapel *by Fra Angelico; the bronze funeral monuments of Sixtus V and Innocent VIII by Antonio del Pollaiolo; the* Palazzo Venezia *and the* Palazzo della Cancelleria *were built.*

With the arrival of the 16th century, Rome was once more its old self, the « caput mundi », and absolute masterpieces were created by the greatest artists of the time: Raphael, Michelangelo, Bramante, Giulio Romano, Baldassarre Peruzzi, the Sangallos, Vignola and many others who, one after the other, took turns in providing the city with unique masterpieces: churches, squares, fountains, palaces and roads of unequalled beauty came into being.

This felicitous period continued throughout the 17th and 18th centuries. The Carraccis (Farnese Gallery), Guido Reni, Guercino worked in Rome. But above all, Gian Lorenzo Bernini, who laid out St. Peter's square and revealed himself as a peerless sculptor (works in the Museo Borghese). In the 19th and 20th centuries the city grew prodigiously in size and new districts, new roads and new social realities were interwined with the old urban fabric.

Cast of Cicero (106-43 B.C.) from Sabbioneta, near Mantua. Museo della Civiltà Romana.

THE ART IN ROME

*I*t is common knowledge that great works of art are more than simply the expression of an artist's technique and individual talent and that they directly reflect the historical situation and the socio-economic and cultural level of the period in which they saw the light. The creator of a work of art is, after all, first and foremost a product of his time, and his personality, his culture and his aesthetic preferences were formed within a determined social ambience. However, while in theory all that is required for the creation of a work of art is a particularly discriminating aesthetic judgement and mastery of the techniques of expression, in reality economic resources and political backing are also generally called for. This is why the history of classic and modern art, where periods of great splendor alternate with others of decadence, closely reflects the historical, economic and political evolution of the societies involved. No wonder then that most of the great art works had a wealthy or powerful client and that many of the most famous artists of all times had to turn to one or more patrons for protection and support. Many great works of art did indeed see the light of day in periods of great economic prosperity, when resources and products were more than sufficient to satisfy the basic requirements and most pressing material needs of the dominant social group or of the entire population. Only wealth that is in excess can be deviated towards the realization of an essentially spiritual need, such as the gratification of aesthetic taste. The opportunity to invest in the construction of a public infra-structure which a particularly favorable socio-economic state of affairs offered, provided a fertile terrain for the artists of the time, who could thus freely express their creativity and talent with outstanding results. Among other things, the installation and realization of great works of art have frequently been used politically as a means of underscoring the economic prosperity achieved, of celebrating the glories or military and civil conquests of a given regime and, if nothing else, at least of making show of personal prestige and adding luster to a family name. The artistic vicissitudes of the city of Rome are in this sense an extraordinary example. The most important monuments in the capital in fact generally date to the most flourishing periods, in an economic and political sense: the ancient Rome of the emperors and military conquest, and the Renaissance and Baroque Rome of the popes and nobles. The relative scarsity in the city of monuments and great works of art dating to the Middle Ages and the period of the communes also depends directly on the fact that, when compared with its precedent and subsequent splendors, the city then found itself in a relatively inauspicious situation. In part, however, this sparsity is a result of the fact that many monuments of that time were restructured in the course of the following centuries. So far, attention has been centered on the political and economic vicissitudes of the city, but art also flourished with the diffusion and development of the Christian religion, whose culture and spiritual and temporal roots lie in Rome. The existence here of the principal seat of the Catholic Church has in fact favored the rise of a great number of religious buildings and particular and inimitable monuments which are scattered throughout the city's urban fabric.

A ship with a wineload cut in limestone (3rd century). Museo della Civiltà Romana.

ANCIENT ROME

It was not until after Hannibal's defeat in the Second Punic War (202 B.C.) that the first structures that were both monumental and of artistic value were erected in Rome. Temples, statues and other kinds of works had, of course, gone up before. But Roman art at this time was still dependent on Greek and Etruscan models and had not yet developed unique identifying features of its own. Moreover, in line with what was stated above, even though the socio-economic conditions of the city were relatively florid, they had not yet attained the level of future centuries. Another fact to keep in mind is that many works of the period prior to the Punic wars were destroyed when the Gauls sacked Rome (390 B.C.).

The first important interventions of an artistic nature in the urban fabric of Rome therefore took place when the **basilicas** were built in the **Forum**. Much of public life in ancient Rome centered on the Forum – the purely economic aspects (shops, warehouses, places for commercial deals), juridical (tribunals for civil and commercial cases), religious (temples and mausoleums), and administrative (the Curie for the meetings of the decurions and the headquarters of the annual magistratures, the Comizi for the assemblies of the voters, the treasury). It was therefore in this part of Rome that the first great monumental edifices went up. Their nature was basically functional for they were inspired essentially by the dictates of absolving a public function. The great basilicas of the Forum, the **Porcia** (built in 184 B.C.), the **Fulvia** (179 B.C.) and the **Sempronia** (170 B.C.), of which barely a trace remains, and the **Aemilia**, funded by the censors M. Emilius Lepidus and M. Fulvius Nobiliores in 179 B.C. and embellished in 78 B.C. by the consul M. Emilius Lepidus, with its imposing remains, were used to settle civil controversies. In structure these buildings, initially spacious and severe, gradually evolved in the following centuries, assuming first the monumental aspect of the Imperial age, then the decorum of the early Christian basilicas and finally the splendor of the Baroque. Religious requirements were fulfilled at the time by the temples built in the Forum Holitorium and the Forum Boarium, including the **temples of the Fortuna Virilis** (2nd cent. B.C.) and **of Vesta** (1st cent. B.C.) which not by chance were set in the area near the Tiber, in the river and port districts of the city with its shipyards and warehouses, always crowded with travelers, foreigners and traders.

The original structures of the principal bridges of ancient Rome also dated to the republican period and attested to the important part played by the crossings of the Tiber in Roman trading economy. Indeed the **Pons Aemilius** (now Ponte Rotto), was erected as early as 179 B.C., followed by the **Pons Milvius** (109 B.C.) and the **Pons Fabricius** (62 B.C.), still intact. Other bridges were then built under the Empire. Very little remains of the buildings that originally constituted the Roman Forum, for the entire zone was rearranged and rebuilt in Imperial times and in the following centuries. The only relatively old building still extant is the so-called « **Mamertine Prison** », the state prison in which political prisoners were kept (Jugurtha, Vercingetorix, etc.). The **Tabularium** is later and its tall facade closed the Forum in the direction of the Capitoline Hill (or Campidoglio). Built in 78 B.C. by the consul Lutatius Catulus to serve as State Archives, it constitutes another valid example of a monumental building erected for civil and administrative scope.

With the creation of the Empire, the style of the monuments and works of art gradually changed and they became more elaborate and refined as a result of the influence of Greek art and themes. Thanks to the wealth that flowed to Rome from all the provinces of the Empire, the city soon acquired a more opulent and monumental aspect, as befitted the capital of a realm that included a large part of the then known world. Conquests furnished Rome with plunder and prized construction material. The multitude of prisoners brought to the city as slaves provided the necessary manpower. This change in quality was manifest not only in the public edifices, but also in the houses and works commissioned by wealthy Roman patricians (such as the **pyramid of Caius Cestius**, the **mausoleum of Galla Placidia** or the **house of Livia**). The extraordinary socio-economical well-being which was spreading throughout the city is confirmed in the monuments by the use of rare and expensive construction materials such as marble and travertine, in substitution of the more humble wood and brick, easier to come by and subject to deterioration. Not by chance is Augustus cited as having found Rome a city of bricks (27 B.C.) and having left it a city of marble when he died (14 B.C.). As the quality on both the artistic and socio-economic levels rose, a change in the social function of the monuments and public works also became evident. The new sumptuous buildings were less the result of the dictates of an administrative and urbanistic nature than they were a means of exalting the power of the Empire, and the military and political glories of the emperors who ordered them to be built. They seem therefore to have been inspired essentially by celebrative motives, even though this does not necessarily mean a change in function or in architectural type. Generally speaking, temples, baths, palaces, and basilicas continued to be built, but they were flanked by triumphal arches, honorary columns, theaters, amphitheaters, obelisks of Egyptian inspiration, and mausoleums in memory of illustrious men.

The most recurrent and significant expression of the aspiration for greatness of the Roman emperors, of their celebrative intentions and of the prosperity the city achieved in the first two centuries of the Empire, was undoubtedly the construction of the **Imperial Forums**. The first to be built was **Caesar's Forum**, erected between 54 and 46 B.C. (still therefore in the period of the republic, but already marked by Julius Caesar's absolutist design) on the slopes of the Capitoline hill, and consisting of a large rectangular enclosure with porticoes and tabernae, and with the temple of Venus, progenitress of the «gens Julia» at the center. Next came the **Forum of Augustus**, centered around the large temple of Mars Ultor, the **Forum of Vespasian or of Peace** (erected after the fall of Jerusalem and the pacification of the East) and that of **Nerva or the Forum Transitorium** (because it joined the two preceding forums and provided a link with the Suburra district). Not much remains today, in part because, as a result of analogous celebrative aims, the zone was cleared away during the Fascist period to make way for the Via dei Fori Imperiali where the assemblies and military parades of the regime took place. **Trajan's Forum**, designed by the great architect Apollodorus of Damascus and constructed between A.D. 112 and 117, was so imposing that in the 2nd century it became a synonym for the heart of public and economic life in the city. In addition to the actual Forum, with its two great hemicycles of porticoes and shops (**Trajan's Markets**), it included the **Basilica Ulpia**, **Trajan's Column**, and the **Temple of Trajan and Plotina**, erected in memory of the emperor by his successor Hadrian.

Other buildings for civil and religious purposes were later built inside the Roman Forum and the Imperial Forum, and while they have in part impaired the original structures, they have also in a certain sense perpetuated its function as a monumental and civic center of the city. The **Basilica Julia** was built by Caesar in the old Roman Forum, and the **Basilica of Maxentius**, terminated by Constantine in the 4th century is still impressive with its three gigantic coffered vaults. Other buildings include the **Temples – of Caesar** (finished in A.D. 29 by Augustus), **of Vesta** (in which the sacred fire, symbol of the eternity of the Roman State was kept), **of Castor and Pollux, of Vespasian** (1st cent.), **of Venus and Roma** (the largest in the city), **of Antoninus and Faustina** (built in the 2nd cent. A.D. and now occupied by the Baroque church of San Lorenzo in Miranda), **of Romulus** (in honor of the Emperor Maxentius' son), and **of Saturn** (4th cent.).

The **Triumphal Arches of Titus and of Septimius Severus** (dating respectively to the 1st and 3rd cent.) also stand in the area of the Forum. Not far away is the **Arch of Constantine**, erected in the 4th century in honor of the victory of Ponte Milvio (A.D. 312). The Roman tradition of the triumphal arch dates to republican times when wooden arches with garlands of oak and laurel were set up to celebrate the return of the victorious armies. Generally placed at the beginning of the most heavily traveled roads, in Imperial times the commemorative and celebrative function was maintained and accentuated, above all in honor of the greatest emperors. Obviously the materials chosen for the construction became more important (marble or stone), the structures more imposing and the decoration richer (even though often taken from precedent works).

The historiated columns, in which the military campaigns of the emperors were celebrated, had an analogous scenographic and commemorative function. The chronological succession of the events sculptured in bas-relief along the entire external course of the decoration is a good illustration of the historical-narrative character of Roman art. This is particularly evident in **Trajan's Column**, erected in A.D. 113 to celebrate his victory over the Dacians, but it also comes to the fore in the **Aurelian Column**, raised to commemorate Marcus Aurelius' triumph over the Germans and the Sarmatians (A.D. 176), and in the remains of the **Antonine Column**, also erected by Marcus Aurelius, in memory of Antoninus Pius (A.D. 161-169).

The same reasoning underlies the **Ara Pacis Augustae** (13 B.C.), the **Pantheon** (initially built by Agrippa, but then rebuilt by Hadrian in A.D. 125), and the great funerary constructions such as the **Mausoleum of Augustus** and **of Hadrian** (A.D. 138, which then became fortress, papal residence and prison.

Theaters too, such as the one dedicated to **Marcellus** (A.D. 11) and built by Augustus, the amphitheaters, first of all the **Colosseum or Flavian amphitheater**, terminated by Titus in A.D. 80, which could contain up to 50.000 spectators, and the **circuses** (such as those of **Domitian**, of **Maxentius**, and above all the **Circus of Flaminius** and that of **Maximus**, with a seating capacity of 300,000) are examples of monumental buildings which express the wealth and grandeur of Rome. The last fundamental component of monumental town planning in Roman times was the **Baths**, a place for physical cure, for rest, but above all a cultural and social center. During the early centuries of the Empire this social and civic function of the Baths was intensified, and more and larger structures were constantly being built. In this case too, the construction of a bath complex became a means by which the emperors could express their power and wealth in the manifest opulence and magnificence of the art and architecture. Frequently plundered and damaged by the various later invaders, the Bath complexes still furnish us with an idea of their past splendor, as in the remains of the **Baths of Trajan** A.D. 110), **of Caracalla** (A.D. 216), and **of Diocletian** (A.D. 298).

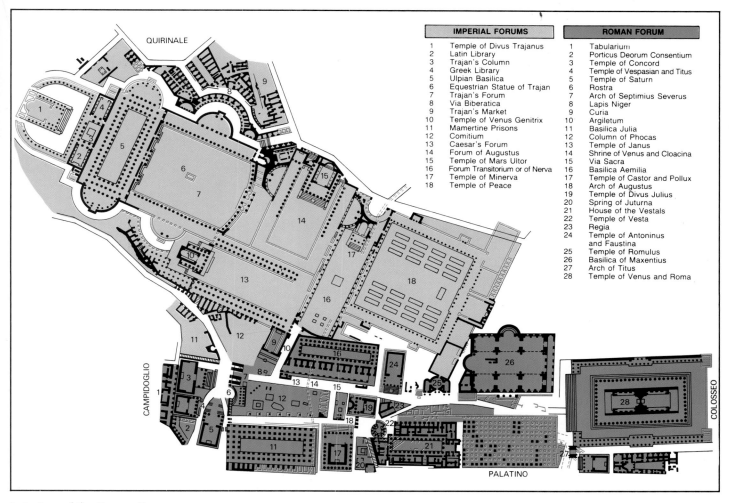

IMPERIAL FORUMS	
1	Temple of Divus Trajanus
2	Latin Library
3	Trajan's Column
4	Greek Library
5	Ulpian Basilica
6	Equestrian Statue of Trajan
7	Trajan's Forum
8	Via Biberatica
9	Trajan's Market
10	Temple of Venus Genitrix
11	Mamertine Prisons
12	Comitium
13	Caesar's Forum
14	Forum of Augustus
15	Temple of Mars Ultor
16	Forum Transitorium or of Nerva
17	Temple of Minerva
18	Temple of Peace

ROMAN FORUM	
1	Tabularium
2	Porticus Deorum Consentium
3	Temple of Concord
4	Temple of Vespasian and Titus
5	Temple of Saturn
6	Rostra
7	Arch of Septimius Severus
8	Lapis Niger
9	Curia
10	Argiletum
11	Basilica Julia
12	Column of Phocas
13	Temple of Janus
14	Shrine of Venus and Cloacina
15	Via Sacra
16	Basilica Aemilia
17	Temple of Castor and Pollux
18	Arch of Augustus
19	Temple of Divus Julius
20	Spring of Juturna
21	House of the Vestals
22	Temple of Vesta
23	Regia
24	Temple of Antoninus and Faustina
25	Temple of Romulus
26	Basilica of Maxentius
27	Arch of Titus
28	Temple of Venus and Roma

◀ A view of the Roman Forum.

Plan of the Imperial Forums and the Roman Forum.

ROMAN FORUM

HISTORY

Situated in a valley between the Palatine, the Capitoline and the Esquiline hills, the area was originally a most inhospitable zone, swampy and unhealthy, until surprisingly modern reclamation work was carried out by the king Tarquinius Priscus, who provided the area with a highly developed drainage system (Cloaca Maxima). Once this complex reclamation work was finished, the Roman forum became a place for trade and barter. Numerous shops and a large square known as the market square were built and a zone was set apart for public ceremonies. It was here that the magistrates were elected, the traditional religious holidays were kept and those charged with various crimes were judged by a real court organization. After the Punic wars, thanks to the extraordinary development of the city, the urban fabric of the Forum took on a new look. As early as the 2nd century B.C., various basilicas — Porcia, Sempronia, and Aemilia — were built, the temples of the Castors and of Concordia were rebuilt, and the network of roads connecting the Forum to the quarters of the city continued to grow. After various transformations under the emperor Augustus, the Roman Forum became so large as to be considered the secular, religious, and commercial center of the city. After a period in which secular and political interests centered on other parts of the city, the Roman Forum reacquired its original prestige under Maxentius and Constantine who ordered the construction of the Temple of Romulus and the great Basilica of Constantine. With the decadence of the Roman Empire, the splendid venerable structures of the Forum were severely damaged by the Barbarian invasions, especially the Goths (A.D. 410) and the Vandals (A.D. 455). The Roman Forum meanwhile became a place of worship for the early Christians who built the Churches of SS. Sergio e Bacco (on the Via Sacra), of S. Adriano (on the Curia), SS. Cosma e Damiano (Temple of Peace). As time passed, the Forum was completely abandoned. What was left of the antique monuments was used by the people or demolished. During the Middle Ages the Forum became a pasture for sheep and cattle (hence its name of Campo Vaccino). For many centuries the prestige of the Roman Forum was a thing of the past. Not until the early 20th century was there a systematic reevaluation of the area with excavation campaigns which lasted for various decades and which brought back to light the splendid evidence of the Rome of the kings as well as that of the republic and of the empire.

Above: a stretch of the Via Sacra with the remains of the Basilica Aemilia in the area between the Curia (on the left) and the Temple of Antoninus and Faustina (on the right). Below: the remains of the Basilica Aemilia with the Temple of Antoninus and Faustina in the background. Facing page: two details of the remains of the Basilica Aemilia.

THE BASILICA AEMILIA

The Basilica Aemilia comprises the long side of the square of the Roman Forum and is fronted to the west by the road of the Argiletum.

The Basilica Aemilia consists of a large hall (m. 70x29) divided into aisles by rows of columns. The nave, about twelve meters wide, is flanked by one aisle on the south and two aisles on the north. There are remains of paving in colored marble. On the side towards the square of the Forum the building was preceded by a two-story portico with sixteen arches on piers. The three columns still standing belong to the reconstruction after A.D. 410. Behind the portico is a series of *tabernae* for bankers, built to take the place of the *tabernae novae*, wiped out in the construction of the basilica. The three entrances that led to the hall are set between them.

Fragments of slabs in marble which belonged to a figured frieze that ran along the architrave of the first interior order have been found in the basilica. The subject matter was concerned with stories relating to the origins of Rome: the *Childhood of Romulus and Remus with Acca Larenzia*, the *Founding of the city*, the *Rape of the Sabines*, the *Killing of Tarpeas* and others.

Two views of the Temple of Antoninus and Faustina, now part of the Church of San Lorenzo in Miranda.

THE TEMPLE OF ANTONINUS AND FAUSTINA

The temple faces onto the Via Sacra, in front of the north side of the Regia to the east of the Basilica Aemilia.
The building has reached us in good condition because the church of S. Lorenzo in Miranda was built inside in the early Middle Ages. The temple, imposing in its size, consists of a cella originally faced with cipolin marble, and placed on a podium, access to which is by a modern staircase, with a brick altar in the center. The pronaos consists of six Corinthian columns on the front and two on each side, in cipolin marble and seventeen meters high, on some of which images of gods are engraved. The frieze has confronting griffins and plant designs.

THE VIA SACRA

Various ancient sources have provided detailed information on the Via Sacra but the entire route followed by this course, which changed along with the history of the city of Rome, has not yet been completely identified. There are various hypotheses regarding the use of the term « Sacra ». Varro tells us it depended on the fact that it was the route taken by the sacred processions while Festus adds the mythical episode of the sacred pact between Romulus and Titus Tatius which tradition locates here. In any case it seems likely that a decisive element in the acquisition of the name is the fact that the oldest and most important places of worship were situated along this route.

15

The square Curia, built entirely in brick.

THE CURIA

The building touches on the southwest side of Caesar's forum of which it is in a sense an adjunct, between the road of the Argiletum and the Comitium.

It represents the seat of the Roman Senate. Tradition attributes the founding of the first permanent Curia to king Hostilius from which it took the name *Curia Hostilia*. It was rebuilt and enlarged in 80 B.C. by Silla but in 52 B.C. it was destroyed in a fire provoked by incidents connected with the funeral of the tribune Clodius. It was then moved from its original site by Caesar who built his Forum there and who began to rebuild the Curia in its present site.

His death in 44 B.C. interrupted work and the new Curia, rebaptised by decree of the Senate *Curia Iulia*, was not finished until 29 B.C. by Augustus, who also erected a portico known as *Chalcidicum*.

After the fire of A.D. 64 it was restored by Domitian in A.D. 94, but it had to be resto-red once more by Diocletian after the fire of Carinus in A.D. 283 and it was then rededicated in A.D. 303.

The ground plan as we have it now dates to this phase even if Honorius I transformed the building in A.D. 630 into the Church of S. Adriano, and it was frequently remodelled and finally torn down between 1930 and 1936 in order to bring to light the important archaeological site.

The building has a rectangular ground plan with four large buttress piers at the external corners, in line with the facades. The main facade has an entrance door and three large windows which illuminate the hall which is 21 meters high, 27 meters long and 18 meters wide, its proportions respecting the Vitruvian canon for curias. It had a flat

Panorama of the Roman Forum with the Arch of Septimius Severus and the Curia.

timber roof and the present one is obviously modern.
Two reliefs known as the *Plutei of Trajan* and found in the central area of the Forum in 1872 are to be seen inside the Curia. They are sculptured on both sides and must have belonged to some unknown monument, perhaps the enclosure of the *Ficus Ruminalis* or the Rostra Anziati.
Both panels have a pig, a sheep and a bull, for the « *souvetaurile* » sacrifice, on one side. The other two sides have two historical friezes which refer to moments in Trajan's reign.
One panel shows Trajan, on the left, escorted by lictors, haranguing the crowd from the Rostra Aziaci in front of the Temple of the Divus Julius. Various monuments in the Forum can be recognized in the background: the Arch of Augustus, the Temple of Castor and Pollux and, beyond the *Vicus Tuscus*, the Basilica Julia, and then the *Ficus Ruminalis*

and the statue of *Marsyas*. Near the center of the relief, the emperor appears once more on a pedestal, seated and flanked by the personifications of *Italia* with a child in her arms, perhaps a statue placed in the square of the Forum to celebrate the liberal imperial measures.
The scene on the other panel illustrates the cancelling of the outstanding debts of the citizens: archive officials bring the registers with the outstanding debts and burn them in the presence of the emperor, in the Forum. Spatially and conceptually this scene is a continuation of the preceding relief, as also shown by the buildings on the same side of the Forum represented in the background. From the left are repeated the *Ficus Ruminalis* and the statue of *Minerva*, then the rest of the eastern side of the Basilica Julia, the *Vicus Iugarius*, the Temple of Saturn, the Temple of Vespasian and Titus, to end up with the Rostra Anziati.

The two sides of the arch of Septimius Severus.

THE ARCH OF SEPTIMIUS SEVERUS

The arch is situated between the Rostra and the Curia and faces onto the square of the Roman Forum on the northeast. It was built in A.D. 203 to celebrate Septimius Severus' two Parthian campaigns of 195 and 197.
The arch is about 20 meters high, 25 meters wide and over 11 meters deep and has three passageways, a large one in the center and two smaller ones at the sides with short flights of steps leading up to them. On top is a tall attic with a monumental inscription which dedicates it to Septimius Severus and his son Caracalla. Representations of the monument on antique coins show that there was once a bronze quadriga with the emperors on the summit.
The arch is built of travertine and brick faced with marble. On the front are four columns standing on tall plinths decorated with reliefs of Roman soldiers and Parthian prisoners. The decoration includes two *Victories*, above *Genii of the Seasons*, which frame the central opening, and *Personifications of Rivers* for the side openings, with a small frieze with the *Triumphal Procession of the emperors* above. Gods are represented in the keystones: *Mars* twice for the principal arch and two female figures and two male figures, one of whom is *Hercules*, on the lesser arches.
But the most interesting part of the decoration is the series of four panels (m. 3.92x4.72) set above the side openings.

The story of the two *Parthian campaigns* unfolds in a series of significant episodes. Each panel should be read from the bottom to the top, beginning with the left-hand panel on the side towards the Forum. Here are represented the phases of the first war, with the departure of the army from an encampment, a *Battle between Romans and Parthians* and the *Freeing of the city of Nisibis* to which the Parthians had laid siege, with the flight of their king Vologases and terminating with a scene of the *Emperor delivering a speech* to his army.
The second panel presents events from the second war: in the lower register the *Roman attack on Edessa* using war machines, including a large battering ram, and the *City opening its gates to surrender*; in the central band *Abgar*, king of Osrhoene, makes the *Act of submission to Septimius Severus* who harangues the army; in the upper tier is shown an imperial *Council of war* in a *castrum* and the *Departure* for enemy territory.
The third panel shows the *Attack on Seleucia*, a city on the Tigris, with the *Fleeing Parthians on horseback*, the *Submission of enemies* to the emperor and his *Entrance into the conquered city*.
And lastly the fourth panel shows the *Siege of the capital, Ctesiphon*, with war machines, and the flight from the city of the Parthian king Vologases and, in conclusion, the *Emperor's speech* before the conquered city.

THE TEMPLE OF SATURN

The temple was pseudoperipteral with Ionic columns on a high podium, situated southwest of the Rostra, on the slopes of the Capitoline hill.

It was one of the oldest temples in Rome and was erected in 497 B.C. but was completely rebuilt in 42 B.C. by the aedile L. Munazius Plancus. The large podium entirely faced in travertine, 40 meters long, 22.50 meters wide and 9 meters high, which is still extant dates to this phase. As indicated by the inscription on the architrave the temple was once more restored in A.D. 238 after a fire.

An avant-corps in front of the base consisted of two podia separated by a flight of stairs which led to the temple. One of these must have contained the headquarters of the Roman State Treasury. The threshold is still to be seen on the side facing the Forum.

The cella of the temple contained the statue of the god which was carried in procession for triumphal rites.

When this temple was built, Rome was passing through a particularly critical period due to extensive famines, epidemics and a severe economic and commercial crisis which characterized the years subsequent to the fall of the monarchy.

Evidence of the sense of distress which took hold of the Roman people is the erection in these years of a number of temples: to Saturn in 497 B.C.; to Mercury, protector of commerce, in 495 B.C.; to Ceres, goddess of the earth and fertility, in 493 B.C.. The building of the Temple to Saturn must also be seen in this light for the god, before being identified with the Greek Cronos, was venerated for a particular characteristic known as « Lua Saturni », in other words the possibility of freeing the city from its afflictions.

◄ What remains of the front part of the Temple of Saturn with the Civil Forum in the background.

Above: a detail of the model of ancient Rome in the Museo della Civiltà Romana, showing the Forum as it was 2000 years ago.

Column of Phocas.

Above: a view of the Civil Forum with the ruins of the Basilica Julia on the right. Below and on the facing page: details of the Basilica.

THE BASILICA JULIA

The basilica comprises the long south side of the Forum and it is bordered on the west by the *Vicus Iugarius* and on the east by the *Vicus Tuscus*, which separate it respectively from the Temple of Saturn and the Temple of the Castors. Work on the building was begun in 54 B.C. by Julius Caesar, from whom it took its name, and it was dedicated in 46 B.C.. The area was previously occupied by the *tabernae veteres* (market shops) and the Basilica Sempronia, built in 169 B.C. by Tiberius Sempronius Gracchus, father of the plebeian tribunes Tiberius and Gaius. At that time the house of Scipio Africanus as well as various shops had had to be torn down.

The Basilica Julia was finished by Augustus but was destroyed in a fire of 14 B.C. and reconstructed by Augustus who dedicated it in A.D. 12 to his adopted sons Gaius and Lucius. The fire of Carinus in A.D. 283 caused considerable damage and Diocletian saw to the restoration. It was once more partially destroyed when Alaric sacked Rome in A.D. 410 and it was reconstructed in A.D. 416 by the prefect of the city, Gabinius Vettius Probianus.

The court of the *Centumviri* was held in the Basilica and it also served as a meeting place for those who frequented the Forum. The building, imposing in size (m. 96x48), was composed of a large central space (m. 82x18) with four aisles around it which were meant to serve as corridors.

They were vaulted and set on two stories with arches framed by engaged columns.

The large central hall must have been divided into four parts by wooden partitions or curtains, so that four courts could carry on business at the same time, although in particularly important cases it was used in its entirety. The only part of the building still extant is the stepped podium, while the brick piers are a modern additon.

Still in place are various pedestals for statues, with inscriptions, three of which name Polykleitos, Praxitiles and Timarchus as sculptors. Various « gaming boards » (*tabulae lusoriae*) had been scratched into the pavement and steps, probably by the idlers who hung around the Forum. There are also *graffiti* sketches of some of the statues which seem to have been nearby.

THE TEMPLE OF CASTOR AND POLLUX

Facing on the square of the Roman Forum to the west of the Arch of Augustus, the temple is separated from the *Vicus Tuscus* by the east side of the Basilica of Gaius and Lucius. The temple was first built here in 484 B.C. and frequently rebuilt and enlarged. Its present aspect is that given to it by Tiberius in A.D. 6. The building was peripteral with eight Corinthian columns on its short sides and eleven on its long sides and with a cella on a concrete base (opus caementicium) (m. 50x30x7) which was originally faced with tufa blocks which were removed in modern times and reused.

The podium we now see dates to the restoration carried out by Metellius in 117 B.C., as do the stretches of black and white mosaic on the paving of the cella.

During the republican period, senate meetings were also held in the temple and after the middle of the 2nd century B.C. the podium also became a tribune for magistrates and orators in the legislative meetings that took place in this part of the forum square. It was from here that Caesar proposed his agrarian reforms. The building also became the headquarters for the office of weights and measures and during the period of the Empire part of the treasury of the tax office was kept in rooms in the long sides.

◄ A picture of the Basilica Julia with the remains of the piers in the foreground; in the background, on the left, the columns of the Temple of Castor and Pollux or Temple of the Dioscuri and a portion of the entablature.

The remains of the colonnade of the Temple of Castor and Pollux with a portion of the entablature.

The podium of the Temple of Divus Julius, with the exedra and the altar in commemoration of Julius Caesar.

The remains of the Temple of Vesta. ▶

THE TEMPLE OF DIVUS JULIUS

The temple is at the eastern end of the Piazza del Foro with the Basilica Aemilia to the north, the Temple of the Castors to the south and the Regia to the east.

It was built in 29 B.C. by Augustus as part of his project for the restructuring of the area of the Roman Forum, in the intent of giving the square a new disposition.

The temple is dedicated to the deified Julius Caesar (it is the first example in Rome) and stands on the site of his cremation after his body had been brought near the Regia, his official residence as Pontefix Maximus. A marble column was erected here in memory of the « father of the country », as stated in the inscription, replaced by a semi-circular exedra with an altar, which opens at the center of the temple podium, on the facade.

The Temple of Divus Julius, of which only the base is still extant, consisted of a cella on a podium, access to which was provided by a flight of stairs on either side. The pronaos had six Corinthian columns on the front and two at the sides and, except for the facade, it was surrounded by a colonnade, to be identified as the *Porticus Iulia*. The rosters taken from the ships of Antony and Cleopatra in the battle of Actium in 31 B.C. seem not, as formerly believed, to have decorated the podium, but were on the front of an orator's tribune which stood in front of the temple.

The building is connected to the Basilica Aemilia by the portico dedicated to Gaius and Lucius, Augustus' grandsons, and to the temple of the Castors (the brothers Tiberius and Drusus) by the Augustan arch of the victory of Actium which was replaced in 19 B.C. by the one of the « Parthian » victory. It therefore belongs to a real propagandistic program in which the emperor's aim was to have the whole square echo with the name of the *Gens Iulia*.

THE TEMPLE OF VESTA

The temple, which is one of the oldest in Rome, is situated to the south of the Via Sacra in front of the Regia. Its present appearance dates to A.D. 191, when it was restored (the last of many restorations) by Giulia Domna, wife of Septimius Severus. This was where the fire sacred to Vesta, the goddess of the household hearth, had to be kept perennially burning, for disaster threatened if the flame were to go out. This obviously meant the building was frequently in danger of fire.

The cult of Vesta goes back to the earliest days of Rome. According to tradition the mother of Romulus and Remus was a vestal virgin, and Livy refers that Numa Pompilius founded the order of the vestal priestesses charged with the care of the temple, establishing a retribution paid by the State and particular privileges.

The building is circular and consists of a cella surrounded by twenty Corinthian columns set on a podium 15 meters in diameter faced with marble and with a staircase leading up to it on the east. The roof was conical with an opening for the smoke. The cella, which was articulated externally by engaged columns, contained no cult statue but only the hearth that was sacred to the goddess.

THE HOUSE OF THE VESTALS

The *Atrium Vestae*, on the south side of the Via Sacra, was a complex consisting of the Temple of Vesta and the house where the vestal virgins lived. As priestesses of the cult of Vesta, they were the custodians of the sacred hearth and were charged with performing the various rites involved. The only feminine body of priests in Rome, the six vestal virgins were chosen among the children of patrician family between six and ten years old. They were required to stay in the order for thirty years, respecting a vow of chastity. On the other hand they enjoyed important privileges: they were subtracted from parental authority and the *patria potestas* passed to the Pontefix Maximus, they could travel in the city in a wagon (which was forbidden to women), they had reserved seats at the spectacles and ceremonies and could do as they best saw fit with a sort of stipend they received from the State.

The entrance to the House of the Vestals is to the west, flanked by an aedicula which probably served as a lararium. It leads into a large rectangular central courtyard around which is a colonnade with eighteen columns on the long sides and six on the short sides, arranged in two orders. The porticoes originally housed the statues which represented the *Virgines Vestales Maximae* (the senior members of the order), many of which have been found in the courtyard together with bases naming them in inscriptions which all date from the time of Septimius Severus on. Some of the statues have been left here, arbitrarily arranged and on pedestals which do not belong to them.

The central part of the east side of the complex is comprised of the so-called « *tablinum* », a spacious hall that was originally vaulted, from which six rooms open off. They were also vaulted and are all about the same size (m. 4.15x3.50) which would lead one to think they were the rooms of the six vestal virgins. This group of rooms is generally thought to be the sanctuary of the Lares and is also where the *statue of Numa Pompilius* which has come down to us may originally have stood.

On the ground floor the south side has a series of service rooms set along a corridor — an oven, a mill, a kitchen, etc. Upstairs are the rooms of the vestals with baths. There must also have been a third floor.

◀ The House of the Vestals.

Above: two statues of priestesses inside the House. Below: the courtyard with the statues originally set under the portico.

◄ The Temple of Divus Romulus.

The remains of the Basilica of Maxentius with its characteristic arches and the Church of Santa Francesca Romana on the right.

THE TEMPLE OF DIVUS ROMULUS

The building faces onto the Via Sacra between the area occupied by the archaic burial grounds and the Basilica of Maxentius. It appears not to have been a temple dedicated to Romulus, deified son of Maxentius, for the building is of Constantinian date and was probably the temple to the Penates which we know originally stood in the area occupied at the beginning of the 4th century A.D. by the Basilica of Maxentius and then transferred to an adjacent site. The building is circular in plan and built in brick. The entrance with its original bronze portal opens at the center of the curved facade. It is framed by two porphyry columns with bases in travertine and marble capitals which support a marble architrave. Four niches for statues are on either side the entrance and two elongated apsed rooms flank the temple. They are preceded by two columns in cipolin marble and must have housed the statues of the Penates.

In the 6th century A.D. the temple became the atrium of the church of SS. Cosma and Damian, originally a large room of the Forum of Peace that lay behind it. One hypothesis identifies this temple with that of Jupiter Stator which has never been localized but which was mentioned in literary sources of Constantinian date together with other buildings on the left of the Via Sacra, whereas no mention is made of the Temple of Divus Romulus.

The imposing arches of the Basilica of Maxentius, still intact.

THE BASILICA OF MAXENTIUS

Access to the Basilica of Maxentius, which stands outside the current archaeological zone of the Roman Forum, is from the Via dei Fori Imperiali. The building was begun in A.D. 308 by Maxentius and finished by Constantine, who modified the internal layout, shifting the entrance from the east to the south side, on the Via Sacra.

The building stands on a platform which is in part a substructure and which is superimposed on storerooms of considerable size, occupying an area of 100 by 65 meters. The entrance in the first plan, which Constantine also retained, opened into a narrow elongated atrium from which three openings led into the large central area, oriented east-west, 80 meters long, 25 meters wide and 35 meters high, covered by three cross vaults supported by eight columns in proconnesian marble, 14.50 meters high, set against piers (none of which are still *in situ*). At the back, right across from Maxentius' entrance, there was a semi-circular apse which contained an enormous acrolithic statue of Constantine (with the uncovered parts of the body in marble and the rest probably in gilded bronze), the head of which, 2.60 meters high, and a foot, two meters long, were found in 1487.

The aisles on either side of the nave were divided into three communicating bays with transversal coffered and stuccoed barrel vaults. Constantine's new project shifted the axis of the basilica from east-west to north-south, maintaining the tripartite division, with an entrance on the south side with four tall porphyry columns and a flight of steps which led from the Via Sacra to the floor of the building which was partly encased in the Velian hill. Across from this entrance a new semi-circular apse was set into the wall at the center of the north aisle, preceded by two columns and with niches for statues framed by small columns on corbels.

The nave was illuminated by a series of large windows in the clerestory while the side aisles had two tiers of arched windows.

The ground plan and dimensions of the building were inspired by the imposing halls of the imperial baths, which were also called « *basilicas* ».

The Baroque facade in travertine of the Church of Santa Francesca Romana with its bell tower.

CHURCH OF SANTA FRANCESCA ROMANA

Built in the second half of the 10th century, the church was remodelled more than once in the course of time. The profiled white **facade** in travertine dates to the early 17th century and is by Carlo Lombardi who was extremely active in Rome at the time. The gabled facade is crowned by statues and has two orders of paired pilasters set on high stylobates. Above there is a large balcony and a porch with three arches.

The single nave **interior** has a fine coffered ceiling and a very old square of Cosmatesque mosaic in the pavement. At the back of the nave is an arch known as the Holy Arch, with a *Confessio* in polychrome marble by Bernini and a shrine with four columns which contains a fine marble group of *Saint Francesca Romana and an Angel* by Giosue Meli (1866). On the back wall of the right transept are two blocks of basalt, protected by a gate, with two imprints which tradition says were made by Saint Peter when he knelt to pray here. On the left wall is the lovely *Funeral Monument of Gregory XI* by Olivieri. The apse is covered with mosaics depicting the *Madonna and Child with Saints Peter and Andrew*; on the high altar is the reputedly miraculous image of the *Madonna and Child* (12th cent.). Descending into the **crypt** we find the mortal remains of the saint at the altar and right across, a fine relief medallion of *Saint Francesca and an angel* by the school of Bernini. Lastly, the **Sacristy** houses rather fine paintings, including the panel of *Santa Maria Nova* (or the *Madonna del Conforto*) dating to the 5th century; a *Madonna Enthroned* by Sinibaldo Ibi from Perugia (1524); an imposing altarpiece, the *Miracle of St. Benedict*, by Subleyras, and various fine paintings by the school of Caravaggio. The adjacent **Convent** is the seat of the **Antiquarium Forense**.

The remains of the Temple of Venus and Roma with the Arch of Titus on the left.

The east facade of the Arch of Titus. ►

THE ARCH OF TITUS

The arch rises in the eastern zone of the forums, south of the Temple of Venus and Roma.

The inscription on the side towards the Colosseum tells us that it was dedicated to the emperor Titus probably after his death in A.D. 81 by his brother and successor Domitian to commemorate the victory in the Judaic campaign of A.D. 70.

The arch has a single passageway, and is 5.40 meters high, 13.50 meters wide and 4.75 meters deep, faced with pentelic marble (with piers in travertine restored by Valadier in 1822) and on the front and back it has four engaged columns with composite capitals. The decorative sculpture on the outside includes two figures of *Victories on globes and with banners* above the archivolt, the *Goddess Roma* and the *Genius of the Roman people*, on the keystones and a frieze in very high relief in the architrave with the *Triumph of Vespasian and Titus over the Jews*.

Inside the arch a panel at the center of the coffered vault contains a relief with the *Apotheosis of Titus*. The panel on the north depicts a procession in which *Bearers of the lictor's fasces* precede the *Emperor who is being crowned by a Figure of Victory*; on the south side the *procession* as it passes through the *porta triumphalis* which is represented in a perspective view.

THE TEMPLE OF VENUS AND ROMA

Begun in A.D. 121 and inaugurated in 135, the Temple of Venus and Roma was designed by Hadrian himself. The building was set within an enclosing double colonnade which left the two principal facades free and which had two entrance propylaea at the center of the long sides. The dimensions (m. 145x100) of the entire ensemble are imposing.

The temple itself had ten columns on the front and nineteen on the sides; it lacked the traditional podium of Roman temples but stood on a stylobate with four steps and consisted of two cellae which were set back to back. Entrance to the cella was via two porches with four columns between the antae. Originally neither cella was apsed and they were covered with a flat timber roof. Their present aspect is the result of restoration effected by Maxentius in A.D. 307, after a fire. The cellae were given apses at the back which contained the cult statues of Venus and of the Goddess Roma while coffered and stuccoed barrel vaults replaced the original ceiling.

A detail of the model of ancient Rome showing the area of the Roman Forum and the Imperial Forums.
In the insert, panorama of the Roman Forum with the remains of the colonnade of the Temple of Saturn in the foreground.

Left and below: Trajan's Column. Above: Via dei Fori Imperiali.

IMPERIAL FORUMS

Although the Imperial Forums built near the precedent Forum of republican times, the underlying concept was more rational and grand. These enormous public squares (80-90,000 sq. meters) were enclosed by porticoes and an equestrian statue of the emperor was often to be found at the center while the square was shut off at the back by an imposing temple. The Imperial Forums were created with the scope of enhancing the prestige of the city and providing the citizens with a place for their markets, from which they could listen to harangues, and where they could participate in religious ceremonies. The first forum built was the **Forum Iulium** (54-56 B.C.), under the auspices of Caesar himself.

Next came the **Forum of Augustus** (31-32 B.C.), the **Forum of Vespasian** or of Peace (71-75), **Nerva's Forum** (A.D. 98) and lastly **Trajan's Forum** (113). After the 6th century, the Forums were com-pletely neglected and began gradually to be destroyed. During the Middle Ages a tiny portion was recuperated and a small district came into being which blended with the other Roman ruins. Most of it however became a mud-field and was rebaptized the zone of the « Pantani » or bogs, and the splendid buildings of Imperial times were destroyed or gravely damaged. Forgotten for centuries, the area was partially urbanized in the Renaissance but not until the 19th century, and above all the 20th, were the remains of this once magnificent architecture brought to light and the Via dei Fori Imperiali created.

TRAJAN'S FORUM

Trajan's Forum extends northwards from Caesar's Forum and is oriented in the same direction. It is perpendicular to the forum of Augustus with which it borders on the west. The last and most imposing of the Imperial forums in Rome, it is the most important public work carried out by

the emperor Trajan and his architect Apollodorus of Damascus. This imposing complex (300 m. long and 185 m. wide) was built between 106 and 113 A.D., financed by the proceeds of the Dacian war that had just been concluded.

The **Basilica Ulpia** which closed off the back of the square has also been excavated only in part. This is the largest basilica ever built in Rome, 17 meters long and almost 60 meters wide, taking its name from the family name of the emperor.

Trajan's Column stands in Trajan's Forum, between the two libraries, behind the Basilica Ulpia and in front of the temple of Divus Trajanus. Dedicated in A.D. 113, it is Doric; altogether it is almost 40 meters high, and at the top there was a statue of Trajan which was lost and replaced by one of St. Peter by Pope Sixtus V in 1587.

The column was meant to serve as the tomb of the emperor and the entrance in the base leads to an antechamber and then a large room which contained a golden urn with Trajan's ashes. The same door on the right leads to a spiral staircase of 185 steps, cut in the marble, which rises to the top of the column.

A continuous frieze moves around the shaft of the column.

About 200 meters long and varying in height from 90 to 125 centimeters, it represents Trajan's two victorious *Dacian campaigns* of A.D. 101-102 and 105-106, separated in the narration by a figure of *Victory* writing on a shield. The **Temple of the Divus Trajanus** and of the Diva Plotina terminates the Forum to the northeast. It was built in A.D. 121 by Hadrian after Trajan's death. Not much is known about this temple which stood on the present site of the Church of S. Maria di Loreto and which must have been of colossal size with eight Corinthian columns on the front and eight on each side, over 20 meters high.

◄ A section of the colonnade of Trajan's Forum with the Markets of Trajan in the background.

Right: the statue of Trajan set up in the Imperial Forums relatively recently. Below: the hemicycle of Trajan's Markets.

Above: Trajan's Markets with the loggia of the Knights of Rhodes. Below: a view of the Markets with the Torre delle Milizie in the background.

TRAJAN'S MARKETS

The construction of Trajan's Forum required the removal of part of the Quirinal hill, and the architect, Apollodorus of Damascus (who built the Forum as well), brilliantly made use of the slopes to realize a unified structural complex. The front of the markets consists of a large hemicycle in brick behind the eastern exedra of Trajan's Forum, echoing its shape and separated from it by a road paved with large irregular polygonal blocks of lava which had been polished. A series of *tabernae* open in the bottom floors; on the upper floor another row of shops are set against the rock of the cut on the hillside. On the ground floor, at the sides of the tabernae, are two large semi-circular halls, with windows and covered by half domes, that may have been used for schools.

The third level of the complex is a road that rises steeply and which was called « Via Biberatica » in the Middle Ages, (*biber* = beverage or *piper* = spices). What with the addition of a basilica, shops and offices, the entire complex consisted of six separate floors.

Above: a modern statue of Augustus placed in the Imperial Forums. Below: the remains of the temple of Mars Ultor in the Forum of Augustus.

THE FORUM OF AUGUSTUS

The **Forum of Augustus** lies between the Forum of Caesar on the west and the *Subura* district to the east. It was later enclosed on the north by the Forum of Trajan and to the south by the Forum Transitorium. It was constructed after costly expropriations on the part of the emperor so that he could free the area which was occupied by private dwellings. The entrance side, to the southwest, adjacent to the eastern side of Caesar's forum, is now under the Via dei Fori Imperiali as is the case with the front part of the square and the colonnades. There were also two secondary entrances at the back of the forum. The **Temple of Mars Ultor** consisted of a cella on a tall podium faced in marble, access to which was via a staircase with an altar at the center and two fountains at its outer edges. It had eight Corinthian columns over seventeen meters high on the front and eight on the long sides while the back was without (*peripteros sine postico*). The inside also had seven columns in two rows along the walls and at the back an apse with the cult statues of *Venus*, *Mars* and the *Divus Iulius*.

THE FORUM OF CAESAR

The **Forum of Caesar**, the first of the great imperial forums, lies northeast of the republican Roman Forum, along the Clivus Argentarius.

The project was planned as an elongated esplanade, 160x75 meters, with porticoes on three sides and the large Temple of Venus Genetrix in the back, a temple which Caesar had vowed before the battle of Pharsalus against Pompey in 48 B.C..

The **Temple of Venus Genetrix** had a single cella on a high podium with a flight of stairs on each side. There were eight Corinthian columns on the front and nine at the sides, in line with the formula of the *peripteros sine postico*. Two square fountains were set in front of the podium. The interior wall of the cella was articulated by six columns on either side. In the back was an apse with the cult statue of Venus Genetrix but the cella also contained other works of art such as paintings by Timomachus of Byzantium. The temple decoration as we know it now dates to Trajan's period.

THE FORUM TRANSITORIUM OR NERVA'S FORUM

This **Forum** takes its name from the fact that it lies between the republican Roman Forum, the Forum of Augustus, the Forum of Caesar, and Vespasian's Temple (or Forum) of Peace. It is superposed on a stretch of the old road of the Argiletum and the long narrow shape (m. 120x45) was dictated by the limited space available, which also explains the absence of an internal portico and the illusionistic device of setting up a row of columns a short distance from the outer wall. Above them was an attic with reliefs illustrating *Myths* connected with Minerva and a frieze with *Scenes of feminine occupations*. On the south side a stretch of the outer wall in blocks of *peperino* and two Corinthian columns, the so-called « *Colonnacce* », are still standing. In the frieze is the *Myth of Arachne* and on the attic a figure of *Minerva*. The short entrance side was curved, while the pronaos of the **Temple of Minerva**, a Corinthian hexastyle on a podium with a tripartite apsed cella, projected from the back.

◄ Part of the colonnade in the Forum of Caesar.

Below: surviving structures in the Forum of Nerva.

48

Left: aerial view of the Colosseum and the Forums. Above: the Colosseum as it was.

Following pages: another view of the Colosseum.

THE COLOSSEUM

The largest amphitheater ever built in Rome and a symbol for Romanism was the work of the Flavian emperors and was therefore called « Amphiteatrum Flavium ». The name Colosseum first came to be used in the Middle Ages and can be traced to the nearby colossal bronze statue of Nero as the sun god which rose up from the site of the vestibule of the *Domus Aurea*.

The emperor Vespasian began the construction of the Colosseum in the valley between the Caelian, Palatine and Esquiline hills, on the site of the artificial lake around which Nero's royal residence was centered and which had been drained for the purpose. Vespasian's intentions were to restore to the Roman people what Nero had tyrannically deprived them of, as well as that of providing Rome with a large permanent amphitheater in place of the amphitheater

of Taurus in the Campus Martius, a contemporary wooden structure erected by Nero after the fire of A.D. 64 but which was no longer large enough.

Work began in the early years of Vespasian's reign and in A.D. 79 the building, which had gone up only to the first two exterior orders with the first three tiers of steps inside, was dedicated. The fourth and fifth tiers were completed by Titus and it was inaugurated in A.D. 80 with imposing spectacles and games which lasted a hundred days. Under Domitian the amphitheater assumed its present aspect and size. According to the sources he added « *ad clipea* », in other words he placed the bronze shields which decorated the attic, adding the *maenianum summum*, the third internal order made of wooden tiers. Moreover he also had the subterraneans of the arena built, after which the *naumachie* (naval battles for which the arena had to be flooded) could no longer be held in the Colosseum, as we know from the sources.

Additional work was carried out by Nerva, Trajan and An-

49

Left: the entrance to the Colosseum. Above: the interior of the arena with the cavea and the subterranean passages.

toninus Pius. Alexander Severus restored the building after it had been damaged by a fire caused by lightning in A.D. 217. Further restoration was carried out by Gordian III and later by Decius, after the Colosseum had once more been struck by lightning in A.D. 250. Other works of renovation were necessary after the earthquakes of A.D. 429 and 443. Odoacer had the lower tiers rebuilt, as witnessed by the inscriptions which we can read with the names of the senators dating from between 476 and 483 A.D. The last attempt at restoration was by Theodoric, after which the building was totally abandoned.

In the Middle Ages it became a fortress for the Frangipane and further earthquakes led to the material being used for new constructions. From the 15th century on then it was transformed into a quarry for blocks of travertine until it was consecrated by Pope Benedict XV in the middle of the 18th century.

The building is elliptical in form and measures 188x156 meters at the perimeter and 86x54 meters inside, while it is almost 49 meters high. The external facade is completely of travertine and built in four stories. The three lower stories have 80 arches each, supported on piers and framed by attached three-quarter columns, Doric on the first floor, Ionic on the second and Corinthian on the third. They are crowned by an attic which functions as a fourth story, articulated by Corinthian pilasters set alternately between walls with a square window and an empty space which once contained the gilded shields. The beams which supported the large canopy (*velatium*) to protect the spectators from the sun were fitted into a row of holes between corbels. The canopies were unfurled by a crew of sailors from Misenum. The arches of the ground floor level were numbered to indicate the entrance to the various tiers of seats in the *cavea*. The four entrances of honor were situated at the ends of the principal axes of the building and were unnumbered, reserved for upper class persons of rank such as

Sections of the cavea with the connecting corridors.

magistrates, members of religious colleges, the Vestal Virgins. The entrance on the north side was preceded by a porch (a small two-columned portico) which led to the imperial tribune through a corridor decorated with stuccoes. The external arcades led to a twin set of circular corridors from which stairs led to the aisles (*vomitoria*) of the *cavea*; the second floor had a similar double ambulatory, and so did the third, but lower than the other two, while two single corridors were set one over the other at the height of the attic.

Inside, the *cavea* was separated from the arena by a podium almost four meters high behind which were the posts of honor. It was horizontally divided into three orders (*maenianum*) separated by walls in masonry (*baltei*). The first two *maeniana* (the second subdivided once more into upper and lower) had marble seats and were vertically articulated by the entrance aisles (*vomitoria*) and stairs. The result are circular sectors called *cunei*. It was therefore possible for the seats to be identified by the number of the tier, the cuneo and the seat. The third *maenianum* (or *maenianum summum*) had wooden tiers and was separated from the *maenianum secundum* below by a high wall. There was a colonnade with a gallery reserved for the women, above which a terrace served for the lower classes who had

The vaulted passageways inside the Colosseum.

standing room only.

Access to seats in the *cavea* was based on social class, the higher up the seat the less important the person. The emperor's box was at the south end of the minor axis and this *was also where consuls and Vestal Virgins sat. The box at the extremity was for the prefect of the city (« praefectus Urbis »)* together with other magistrates. The tiers closest to the arena were reserved for senators. The inscriptions to be read on some of the extant tiers inform us that they were reserved for specific categories of citizens.

The arena was originally covered with wooden flooring which could be removed as required. In the case of hunts of ferocious animals the spectators in the *cavea* were protected by a metal grating surmounted by elephant tusks and with horizontally placed rotating cylinders so that it was impossible for the wild animals to climb up using their claws. The area below the arena floor contained all the structures necessary for the presentation of the spectacles: cages for the animals, scenographic devices, storerooms for the gladiators' weapons, machines, etc. They were arranged in three annular walkways with openings that permitted the areas to be functionally connected with each other. A series of thirty niches in the outer wall was apparently used for elevators which took gladiators and beasts up to the level of the arena.

The artificial basin created for the lake of the Domus Aurea was rationally exploited in the construction of the Colosseum, saving an enormous amount of excavation work. Once drained, the foundations were cast and travertine piers were set into a large elliptical concrete platform, forming a framework up to the third floor with radial walls in blocks of tufa and brick set between them. It was thus possible to work on the lower and upper parts at the same time, so that the building was sub-divided into four sectors in which four different construction yards were engaged simultaneously.

Various types of spectacles were given in the Colosseum: the *munera* or contests between gladiators, the *venationes*, or hunts of wild beasts and the previously cited *naumachie* which were soon transferred elsewheres because of

Above: the model in the Museo della Civiltà Romana of the cross-section of the arena in the Colosseum, in which the cages and subterranean passageways for the wild beasts can be identified. Below: a terracotta slab of Roman date depicting the arena and a hunting scene.

Right: two details of the mosaics from ▶ Tusculum (3rd cent. A.D.) in the Museo Borghese, depicting a hunt (*venatio*) and a duel between gladiators (*munera*).

PVRPVREVS·ENTINVS ~ BACCIBVS

The Colosseum with the columns of the Temple of Venus and Roma in the foreground; a stretch of the paved road in front of the Colosseum.

Facing page: another view of the Colosseum.

the difficulty of flooding the arena of the amphitheater. Titus' reconstruction of the naval battle between Corinth and Corcyra in which 3000 men were employed was famous. The gladiator contests took place in the form of a duel between opposing sides, generally until the death of one or the other. In the *venationes* those condemned to various penalties had to fight wild beasts and they were often unarmed. Records of the bloody outcome of these spectacles is to be found in the writings of ancient authors with reference to 10,000 gladiators and 11,000 wild beasts employed by Trajan on the occasion of his triumph over the Dacians or the impressive number of beasts in the hunts organized by Probus for his triumph.

Christians may or may not have been martyrized in the Colosseum. In A.D. 397 Honorius emanated an edict which prohibited gladiatorial games, but they were renewed under Valentinianus III. From A.D. 438 on, only hunts were allowed, which gradually diminished in importance until the last hunt held in A.D. 523 under Theodoric. A final point to consider is the number of spectators the Colosseum was capable of containing: opinions vary but the figure must have been around 50,000.

The facade of the Arch of Constantine. Right: view with the four marble columns and the Colosseum in the background.

Following pages: two details of the side passageways of the Arch with the statues of the Dacians and the Hadrianic medallions.

CONSTANTINE'S ARCH

The largest of the arches erected in Rome is on the route which the triumphal processions took in antiquity, between the Caelian and the Palatine hills. It is 21 meters high, almost 26 meters wide and over 7 meters deep, with three passageways, the central one of which is larger. It was built in A.D. 315 by decree of the Senate and the Roman people to celebrate the 10th anniversary of Constantine's ascent to the throne and his victory over Maxentius in the battle of Ponte Milvio in A.D. 312. The decoration of the arch employed a number of reliefs and sculpture from other monuments. The four detached marble columns on each of the principal sides, surmounted by eight statues of Dacians, are in *pavonazzetto* marble (white with purple veining, from Asia Minor) and date to Trajan's time. Eight tondos about two meters in diameter of Hadrian's period are set in pairs over the side passageways, inserted into porphyry slabs. Four *Scenes of the hunt* are represented, and four *Sacrificial scenes*. The figure of Hadrian appears in each scene, even though his head has been replaced by

that of Constantine. On the attic, on either side of the inscription which is repeated both on the front and the back of the monument, are eight reliefs from the period of Marcus Aurelius, also set in pairs, which probably came from an honorary arch. They form a cycle which celebrates the *Return of the emperor* in A.D. 173 after his campaigns against the Marcomanni and the Quadi, in a series of exemplary episodes which correspond to scenes presented in the Aurelian column. A large marble frieze from Trajan's time has also been reused. It has been cut into four parts, two of which are on the short sides of the attic and two on the interior of the central passage. The scenes represented have to do with Trajan's two *Dacian campaigns* (A.D. 101-102 and 105-106). The decorative parts which date to the building of the arch comprise the reliefs at the bases of the columns, the keystones of the arches and, on the short sides, medallions with the *Sun God* and the *Goddess of the Moon* on a chariot. The most important part of Constantine's decoration is however the large historical frieze set above the lesser openings, and which continues on the short sides of the arch with episodes from the *Military Deeds* of Constantine.

The so-called Stadium of the Domus Augustana
on the Palatine.

Above: what remains of the Domus Flavia. Below: an allover ►
view of the model of the Palatine.

THE PALATINE

This is the most famous of Rome's hills and it retains the earliest memories of the old city. In fact the first groups of huts of the square city were built on the Palatine, before they spread over to the adjacent hills. Important public buildings, large temples and many private dwellings such as those of Cicero, Crassus and Tiberius Graccus went up here. Later the hill became the residence of the emperors of Rome who had their sumptuous palaces built here, including the **Domus Augustana**, the **Domus Flavia**, the **Domus Transitorio**, the **Domus Aurea**, and the **Domus Tiberiana**, of which considerable remains are still extant. The Palatine was then the residence of the Gothic kings and of many popes and emperors of the Western Empire; in the Middle Ages convents and churches were built. Finally in the 16th century most of the hill was occupied by the immense structures of **Villa Farnese** and the **Orti Farnesiani** (the first real botanical gardens). Archaeological excavation was begun in the 18th century and evidence of Rome's past was brought to light, including remnants of the **Domus Augustana**, the splendid paintings of republican period and the remains of the first dwellings that stood on the hill, as well as the imposing 16th-century entrance portal to the Orti Farnesiani.

Above: the Circus Maximus as it is now. Left: a 1st-century cast in the Museo della Civiltà Romana with a charioteer who has won the race.

THE CIRCUS MAXIMUS

Now only the lay of the land, much higher than the original arena, betrays the form of the original structure. For a long time it was built entirely of wood. In 329 B.C. the *carceres* or stalls for the horses and chariots were built in painted wood, as well as the *spina* in the center which covered and channeled the stream which ran through the valley and around which the race was run.

In 174 B.C. the censors Fulvius Flaccus and Postumius Albinus had the *carceres* built in masonry, and placed seven stone eggs along the spina as markers for the number of circuits the chariots had run. In 33 B.C. Agrippa had bronze dolphins set up for the same scope. Caesar also used the Circus for hunts. On the side towards the Palatine, Augustus had the *pulvinar*, a sacred box reserved for the tutelary gods of the games, set up and in 10 B.C. he had the obelisk of Ramsetes II taken at Heliopolis placed on the spi-

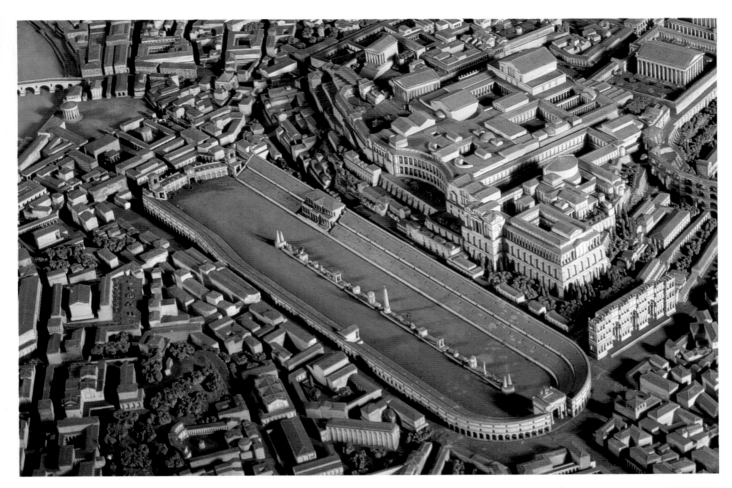

Above: reconstruction of the Circus Maximus in the Museo della Civiltà Romana, where the cast on the right (1st cent. A.D.), depicting a phase in the Circus races, is also to be found.

na. The obelisk, 23.70 meters high, was transferred to Piazza del Popolo by Pope Sixtus V in 1587.

Claudius took a hand in the restoration after a fire in A.D. 36. He had the *carceres* rebuilt in marble and had the *metae* (the goals, conical extremes of the *spina*) covered in gilded bronze. The Circus was once more destroyed in the fire of A.D. 64. Nero rebuilt it and increased the number of seats. Another fire under Domitian ravaged the building and reconstruction was finished by Trajan.

Constantine restored it and Constantius II embellished the *spina* with a second obelisk of Tuthmosis II, which came from Thebes and was even higher than the other one (32.50 m.) and which Pope Sixtus V had placed in Piazza San Giovanni in Laterano in 1587.

The Circus measured 600x200 meters and had a capacity of 320,000 spectators who watched the chariot races that were held there. The most important were those of the *Ludi Romani* the first week of September, which opened with a religious procession in which the highest religious and civil authorities of the city took part.

Above: the entrance to the ruins of the Baths of Caracalla. Left: a two-color mosaic pavement with dolphins inside the Baths. Right, above: the central building and, below, the interior of the Baths.

BATHS OF CARACALLA

The Baths of Caracalla are the most imposing and best preserved example of thermae from the Imperial period still extant. They were built by Caracalla beginning in A.D. 212. In the 16th century excavations carried out in the enormous building brought to light various works of art including the *Farnese Bull* and the *Hercules*, now in the National Museum of Naples. *Mosaics with athletes*, which decorated the hemicycles of the large side courtyards of the thermae, were discovered in 1824 (Vatican Museums).

In their ground plan the Baths of Caracalla clearly distinguished between the actual bath sector and the surroundings where all the accessory non-bathing services were located. At present the central building is accessible and the itinerary is quite like that followed in antiquity by the bathers. The vestibule leads on the right into a square chamber, flanked by two small rooms on either side, covered with barrel vaults. This was the *apodyterium* (dressing-room). Next came one of the two large palaestrae from where the bathing itinerary generally started after various sports and exercises had been done in the palaestra. From here one went to a *laconicum* (turkish bath), the imposing *calidarium* (hot bath) and the *tepidarium* (temperate bath), a more modest rectangular chamber flanked by two pools. Next came the large central hall, the *frigidarium*. The *natatio*, which could also be reached from the *frigidarium*, was uncovered. It has a fine front elevation with groups of niches between columns, once meant to contain statues.

The Pyramid of C. Cestius, of obvious Egyptian inspiration.

Porta San Paolo (the ancient Porta Ostiense) in the circuit of ▶
the Aurelian Walls.

PYRAMID OF C. CESTIUS

The funeral building dating to the early imperial period was obviously inspired by Egyptian models, of the Ptolemaic rather than Pharaonic period, fashionable in Rome after the conquest of Egypt (30 B.C.). The base measures 29.50 m. on each side and the pyramid is 36.40 m. high. On the west side is a small door that leads into the funeral chamber, a hollow in the concrete core which has a rectangular ground plan (m. 5,85x4) and is covered with a barrel vault and faced with *opus latericium*, a facing of brick. The wall was then plastered and richly painted in the so-called third Pompeian style. Interest has centered on the building ever since the Middle Ages when it was called « *Meta Remi* ». An inscription placed on the monument records the fact that in 1660 Pope Alexander VII authorized the excavation. Four antique inscriptions, one on the east side, one on the west, and two engraved on the pedestals which supported the bronze statues of the deceased (in the Capitoline Museums), document the public offices and the heirs of the man for whom the tomb was made.

PORTA S. PAOLO

What is now known as Porta S. Paolo is one of the best preserved city gates (the other is the Porta S. Sebastiano) in the imposing circuit of the Aurelian Walls. Its original name was Porta Ostiensis and as usual this was derived from the name of the road which started at the gate. Despite this, the oldest route followed by the Via Ostiense, the road that led to the great seaport of Rome, ran through a postern south of the Pyramid of Cestius, which was already closed in the time of Maxentius. The current name of the gate derives from the large Early Christian Basilica of S. Paolo fuori le Mura, about two kilometers away. Originally the gate had two entrances framed by semicircular towers. Under Maxentius (A.D. 306-312), two pincer walls with a counter gate were added, also with two passageways in travertine. Under Honorius (395-423), the two passageways of the main entrance became one and the towers were raised. It was through this gate that Totila's Goths entered Rome in 544 during the Gotho-Byzantine was. The rooms inside the building now house the Museo della Via Ostiense.

FORUM BOARIUM

The ancient monuments still visible in this area include two exceptionally well-preserved temples which lie fairly close together in what is now the Piazza Bocca della Verità, corresponding to the old Forum Boarium. The first is known as the **temple of Fortuna Virilis** but should instead be identified as the Temple of Portunus, an ancient tutelary deity of the port. The building stood very close to the *Portus Tiberinus*; just outside the *Porta Flumentana*, and may have been built as early as the period of the kings. It was obviously restored more that once and the present aspect dates to a restoration of the 1st century B.C. The temple stands on a podium in rubblework faced with slabs of travertine. The temple is Ionic pseudoperipteral with four columns on the facade and with the long sides comprised of two columns and five engaged columns on the wall of the cella. The walls of the building are built completely of Aniene tufa. The columns, the bases and the capitals of the engaged columns are in travertine. The entire structure was stuccoed. The original cornice which still preserves the lion protomes is

The Temple of Fortuna Virilis (or Temple of Portunus).
Below: a panorama of the Forum Boarium.

exceptional.

The second temple is the circular structure erroneously indicated as the **Temple of Vesta**. It was, instead, as proved by the discovery of a block inscribed with topographical data, the Temple of Hercules Victor, mentioned in the sources. The building was founded at the end of the 2nd century B.C. by a Roman merchant who had made his fortune in oil. He dedicated the temple to the patron god of the corporation of the *olearii* (Hercules) and had it built near the trading port. The temple is a round peripteral building with twenty Corinthian columns, standing on a stepped crepidoma. The circular cella had an opening on the east. The entablature has been completely lost. The entire building was constructed in Pentelic marble, probably by the Greek architect Hermodoros of Salamina, who had various commissions in Rome in the second half of the 2nd century B.C. The cult statue of the god, called *Hercules Olivarius*, was also by a Greek sculptor, Scopas Minor. As it is now, the building also includes a considerable amount of restoration of the Tiberian age, which involved nine columns and eleven capitals which were remade in luna marble.

The so-called Temple of Vesta (Temple of Hercules Victor).

ISOLA TIBERINA

According to an old written tradition, the small island in the Tiber now known as Isola Tiberina was formed when the grain that had been harvested in the Campus Martius (private property of the Tarquins) was thrown into the river after the expulsion of the Etruscan kings from Rome.

The first important building erected on the island dates to 291 B.C.. This was the temple of Aesculapius.

Nothing remains today of the original building but the site is probably that of the 17th-century **Church of S. Bartolomeo**, and the well that still exists near the altar could correspond to the sacred fount. The porticoes of the sanctuary of Aesculapius were a real hospital. Numerous inscriptions preserved mention miraculous healings or dedications to the god. In the Middle Ages the island continued to be set aside as a hospital, thanks in part to its being isolated from the inhabited areas, and it is still used as such with the **Hospital of the Fatebenefratelli**, adjacent to the small **Church of S. Giovanni Calibita**.

In antiquity the island was also joined to the city by two bridges. The one which still today connects it to the left bank, near the theater of Marcellus, is the ancient **Pons Fabricius**.

The Pons Fabricius is 62 m. long and 5.50 m. wide; the two large slightly flattened arches have a span of 24.50 m. and spring from a massive central pier, which is pierced by a small arch that serves to relieve the pressure of the water on the structure during floods.

The other bridge which joins the island to Trastevere is no longer the original one. The Pons Cestius was torn down between 1888 and 1892. It had been built in the first century B.C., perhaps by the praetor of 44 B.C., the same C. Cestius to whom the famous funeral monument in the shape of a pyramid is dedicated. In A.D. 370 it was restored by emperor Valentinian I.

The unique form of the Isola Tiberina in the shape of an elongated boat, together with the remembrance of the ship which had brought the serpent of Aesculapius to Rome, gave rise to an odd architectural adaptation of the site which probably dates to the first century. The easternmost point of the island was turned into the prow of a trireme.

THEATER OF MARCELLUS

The project for the so-called theater of Marcellus dates to Caesar's time, but the building was finished in 13 B.C. by Augustus who officially dedicated it in the name of his nephew Marcellus, his first designated heir, who died early in 23 B.C.

In the 13th century the building was occupied by the noble Savelli family; in the 18th century it passed to the Orsini. The fine Renaissance palace that occupies the third floor of the exterior facade of the *cavea* is the work of the architect Baldassarre Peruzzi.

The theater must have been built on powerful substructures, and the front was provided with a facade of 41 arches, framed by engaged columns, on three floors. The first two floors are Doric and Ionic orders, the third, of which nothing remains, must have been an attic closed by Corinthian pilasters. It was originally 32.60 m. high.

It has been calculated that the *cavea* (diam. 129.80 m.) could hold between 15 and 20,000 spectators, making it the largest theater in Rome as far as audience capacity was concerned. Beyond the orchestra (diam. m. 37) was the stage, of which nothing remains. On either side were apsed halls, of which a pier and a column of one are still standing. Behind the stage was a large semi-circular exedra with two small temples. The building was also noticeable for its rich decoration, still visible in the Doric frieze on the lower order.

◄ The Isola Tiberina as it is now; in the background the old Pons Fabricius (Ponte Fabricio).

The facade of the Theater of Marcellus, begun by Julius Caesar. The third floor was built in the Renaissance by Baldassarre Peruzzi.

Above: the propylaeum of the Porticus of Octavia. Right: the Synagogue. Facing page, above: Porta Maggiore or Prenestina; below: the remains of the Mausoleum of Augustus.

Following pages: view by night, with Trajan's Column and a section of the dome of the Church of the Santissimo Nome di Maria in the foreground; in the background the monumental complex of the Altare della Patria.

SYNAGOGUE

The **Synagogue**, or Israelite Temple, stands on the Via del Portico di Ottavia, along the Tiber. Like other Italian synagogues, it is characterized by a style that can be classified as exotic revival, in this case Assyro-Babylonian. The building terminates in a large alluminum dome, which marks it as belonging to the early twentieth century. In fact the Synagogue dates to 1904 and was designed by the architects Armanni and Costa.

PORTA MAGGIORE

One of the most monumental signs of Imperial Rome has also given its name to the piazza that came into being around it. Known also as Porta Prenestina and Labicana, it was built in the year 52 by the emperor Claudius, and served as an intersection in which two roads met, one of which led to Preneste and the other to Labici. Architecturally it consists of two openings with the arches flanked by robust piers and aedicules.

PORTICUS OF OCTAVIA

The site of the portico is in the Campus Martius, north of the Theater of Marcellus and the Circus Flaminius (of which nothing remains today).
The complex, built by Augustus between 33 and 28 B.C. and dedicated to his sister Octavia, stands on the site of the Porticus Metelli.
The Porticus of Octavia was destroyed by the fire of A.D. 80 and restored by Domitian. A second reconstruction was undertaken by Septimius Severus after another fire in A.D. 191. The extant remains are of this latter date but the ground plan is provided by the *Forma Urbis* of Severian date.

MAUSOLEUM OF AUGUSTUS

The dynastic tomb of the first emperor of Rome is a circular structure consisting of a series of concentric walls in tufa connected by radiating walls. The first accessible chamber was at the end of the long entrance corridor (*dromos*). Two entrances in this wall lead to the annular corridor which rings the circular cella.
At the center is a pier inside which is a square chamber. The tomb of Augustus was here, in correspondence to the bronze statue of the emperor which was at the top of the pier. The three niches of the cella contained other tombs of important members of the Julio-Claudian dynasty.

CHRISTIAN ROME

*A*t least in the beginning, Early Christian art in Rome did not introduce anything new into the traditional context of late Roman art, except for the insertion of various iconographical elements related to the cult (sacred images). In this first phase, in fact, the need to worship clandestinely was certainly not conducive to the creation of buildings of artistic and architectural note. Christianity, moreover, found its adherents above all among the slaves and the populace, who lacked the resources required for important constructions. The rites and meetings therefore took place in the catacombs, or in the houses provided by wealthy owners who had been converted, or in structures built on their land with whatever was available («Domus ecclesiae»). After the edict of Constantine in A.D. 313, which recognized the right to profess the Christian faith, the first great religious buildings were erected. Their construction also corresponded to the need of organizing the religious practices and sites of worship in a functional and hierarchical manner. The more important churches («Tituli») went up in correspondence to the various Christian communities, structured much like modern parishes. In this early, still tentative phase of the development of Christianity these buildings were in part also motivated by the requirements of apostolate and the desire to bring the activities heretofore practiced in the catacombs out into the open. The architectural model adopted had already been tried and proven. Both in plan and in exterior appearance the new structures resembled their predecessor, the pagan basilica used for civic purposes. In response to popular demand and accellerating religious ferments, the great **basilicas of St. Peter and St. John**, the original remains of which have been found in the buildings that were later erected to replace them, **of St. Paul outside the Walls**, and of the **SS. Apostoli**, were built as early as the 4th century. Next to these great monumental basilica complexes which were used as places of worship and meeting, smaller structures also rose, often in correspondence to the site where, at the dawn of Christianity, some saint or illustrious person had been martyred. Their purpose was therefore essentially commemorative, such as a

Mausoleum, but sometimes they were used for specific rites, such as baptism. They were generally more varied in form and structure than the basilicas, with a ground plan that might be circular (such as the Mausoleum of S. Costanza or of S. Elena), polygonal or cruciform.

The construction of the early Christian basilicas also continued in the following centuries, evidence of the ever greater role played by religious and spiritual life. In the 5th century the **basilicas of S. Maria Maggiore, S. Sabina, S. Lorenzo fuori le Mura, S. Pietro in Vincoli**, etc. were built, followed by **S. Maria in Cosmedin** and **SS. Cosma and Damiano** (6th cent.), **S. Agnese fuori le Mura** (7th cent.), **S. Cecilia in Trastevere** (9th cent.), etc.

The decline of the city of Rome went hand in hand with the economic, political and social crisis of the Empire, until it reached its nadir in the «Gothic war» (A.D. 535-553). The population, decimated by wars, epidemics and famine, sank to less than 50,000 persons (at the height of the Empire in the 2nd century A.D. it was more than a million), while many of the productive activities disappeared and the administrative, civic and political structures also were wanting. Rome survived this period of almost total collapse thanks to the ascent of the Papacy and the choice of Rome as the spiritual capital of the Christian world. Art and culture also reflected the beneficial influences of this rediscovery of the functions of the city. The imposing structures of the Empire, abandoned, dismantled, and fallen into ruin due to lack of maintenance and Barbarian invasions, were replaced by other monumental structures in the urban fabric, erected as a definitive confirmation of the new role the city had assumed in politics and religion. Obviously the repercussions of the economic, demographic and social crisis continued to be felt for some time and were reflected in the relative modesty of the new buildings when compared with the old. As far as materials were concerned, too, of necessity choice generally fell to brick, cheaper and easier to come by, or to reused marble and fine stone, recuperated from constructions dating to Imperial times, which thus were turned into veritable quarries in the heart of the urban fabric. The degradation and the disappearance of so many structures is due in much greater measure to this recurrent practice than to the damage inflicted by the hordes of plundering invaders. The most striking example of this type of continuous hemorrhage is the Colosseum. Its structures have to a large extent been despoiled and as late as the 18th century Pope Benedict XIV was forced to emanate a specific ordinance to avoid its total destruction.

On the other hand the relative poverty of the exteriors was counterbalanced by the splendor of the interior decoration. Sculpture and, above all, mosaics achieved particularly brilliant results, with the former creating a skilful play of lights and darks, and the latter of glittering colors.

As time passed the bishop of Rome was to all extents and purposes the only authority capable of exercising any real function in the city, not only on a spiritual level, but also from the political and administrative point of view, and as early as the 8th century the bases for the exercise of temporal power by the popes was already being laid. It was not long before the most powerful noble families in Rome centered their attention on this augmented political and administrative role of the highest religious organ of Christianity, hoping to maintain exclusive rights to the pontificate and the economic and political advantages to be gained there from. One of the results of the internal struggles which developed in the city was the spread of **tower-houses**, such as that of **Cola di Rienzo** (12th cent.), of the **de' Conti**, and the **Torre delle Milizie** (13th cent.).

Economic conditions improved by degrees as the temporal power of the popes was gradually extended and Rome became the capital of a rich and powerful state (at least in the frame of reference of the contemporary Italian political panorama), as well as respected for the charismatic figure of the Pope. The economic well-being of the Papal State was reflected in the renewed artistic fervor which spread through-out the city thanks above all to the popes and the great Roman families which took turns in electing their members to the papal throne, acquiring wealth and honor.

In the course of the 12th and 13th centuries, while the Tuscan and Lombard Romanesque style was spreading throughout the rest of Italy, in Rome «Cosmati» art was gaining a foothold, characterized above all by the skilful use of polychrome stone inlay, thanks to the talented stone cutters and architects of local origin.

The interests of the various popes in restoration and renewal in the fields of economy, administration, town planning, building and art succeeded in recuperating a great number of buildings, both structurally and functionally. For example the Campidoglio was restored, and a new Senate was installed inside, albeit with powers notably restricted by the Roman Curia and feudal privileges. The socio-economic and cultural development of the city was still limited to a large extent by the continuous wars against the invaders and against the populations intolerant of the temporal power, and by the intestine struggles between the great baronial families, the new-born Comune, soon deprived of its authority, and the papal government. The social structure of the city in fact was characterized on the one hand by the presence of a few noble families, relentlessly struggling against each other but rich enough to destine part of their wealth to the construction of towers and palaces, and on the other by an abundant proletariat living at a subsistence level and exposed to raids, injustice, dearth and famine. It was only thanks to the ambitious projects of Pope Nicolas V, who was the first to conceive the idea of trasforming Rome into a new capital worthy of the Universal Church, and of Julius II, to whose court the greatest artists of the period were called (Bramante, Michelangelo, Raphael, etc.), that in the Renaissance Rome once more became the major center of Italian artistic life, a role it had already held in antiquity. During the reign of the more enlightened popes, the city was radically renewed in its monumental and urban aspects: the monuments and works of art of precedent periods were in part restructured in accordance with the current taste, or were even torn down to make room for the new scenographic and aesthetic exigencies. Many religious buildings, including the great basilicas of St. Peter and of St. John in Lateran, were transformed and rebuilt in line with new projects, which however were not to be terminated until many years later, and with the collaboration of numerous artists. As far as St. Peter's is concerned, for example, the direction of the works was taken over by such well known architects as Bramante, Raphael, Michelangelo, Carlo Maderno, etc., until in the Baroque the Piazza and the Colonnade were definitively installed by Bernini.

At the same time new churches, cloisters, convents, fountains and palaces were also going up, such as the **complex of the Vatican palaces**, the **churches of S. Maria del Popolo** (B. Pontelli 1472-1477), **of the Gesù** (Vignola 1568-1575), of **S. Agostino** (G. da Pietrasanta 1479-1483), of **S. Pietro in Montorio** with the splendid **tempietto by Bramante** (1503), etc.

View of San Pietro's Piazza and Basilica.

The window overlooking Piazza San Pietro ►
where the pope is used to appear.

VATICAN CITY

HISTORICAL SKETCH

Vatican City spreads out to the right of the Tiber and lies between Monte Mario to the north and the Janiculum to the south. Of old the area now covered by the small Vatican State was called Ager Vaticanus and it was occupied by a circus and Nero's gardens. Since 1929, the year in which the Lateran Treaty was stipulated between the Holy See and the Italian State, the Vatican City has been an independent sovereign state and it contains exceedingly important examples of art and architecture. The boundaries of this state, whose residents can be numbered in the hundreds, is defined by the Via Porta Angelica, Piazza del Risorgimento, Via Leone IV, the Viale Vaticano, Via della Sagrestia, and the Piazza San Pietro.

The Pope, in addition to being the head of the Apostolic Roman Catholic Church, has full legislative, executive and judiciary powers. The Vatican State is completely independent of the Italian state, even though they maintain extremely friendly relations. The Vatican prints its own stamps, has its own railroad station, and a well-known newspaper, the Osservatore Romano, which is distributed throughout Italy. The city also has its own police force (once called Pontifical Gendarmes) and a real police service as represented by the famous « Swiss Guards » which, from the early 16th century, protected the person of the pope and still today wear uniforms that were probably designed by Michelangelo.

Two views of the Basilica of San Pietro with the scenic artery of the Via della Conciliazione.

Following page: Piazza San Pietro with Bernini's colonnades and the obelisk seen from the Basilica.

PIAZZA SAN PIETRO

The fact, alone, that the great and truly unique Basilica of San Pietro in Vatican faces out on this square would make it perhaps the most widely known of Roman piazzas. But above and beyond this, the space itself merits attention for its size (an enormous ellipse whose greatest diameter measures 240 m.) and the brilliant project by Gian Lorenzo Bernini whose scope was that of singling out this square from all others through the use of the imposing porticoes. These porticoes are arranged in semicircles along the short sides of the square and consist of four parallel rows of Tuscan-Doric columns which provide a choice of three paths. Above the canonic entablature are 140 colossal statues of *Saints*, as well as the insignia of the patron pope, Alexander VII. At the center of the square, the plain obe-

lisk, flanked by two fountains, stands at the crossing of the two diameters of the ellipse. Termed « aguglia » (needle) in the Middle Ages, the *obelisk* came from Heliopolis and was brought to Rome by the emperor Caligula, and set on the spina of Nero's Circus, which is where San Pietro's in Vatican now stands. Throughout the various phases of restoration, destruction, and reconstruction, the « aguglia » stayed next to the Basilica and was not set up at the center of the square until 1586 by Domenico Fontana, who also saw to the engineering aspect of the undertaking. The other architect, Carlo Fontana, designed the left-hand *fountain* in Piazza San Pietro, built in 1677 as a *pendant* to the one on the right designed by Carlo Maderno about fifty years earlier. A curious fact concerning the obelisk mentioned above is that it was used, or was believed to have been used in the Middle Ages, as a reliquary for the ashes of Caesar, and then (up to now) for a fragment of the Holy Cross.

Detail of the entablature that runs along over the semicircular colonnades set on either side of Piazza San Pietro, crowned by statues of saints and the coat of arms of Pope Alexander VII.

Right: the facade of the Basilica with the Obelisk, brought ▶ from Heliopolis, set at the center of the square by Pope Sixtus V.

BASILICA OF SAN PIETRO

In the classical period the site was occupied by Nero's Circus, between the Tiber, the Janiculum, and the Vatican hill, and San Pietro, the Prince of the Apostles, was martyred and then buried here. Pope Anacletus had already had a small basilica, *ad corpus*, or a simple shrine built here. In 324 the emperor Constantine replaced the presumably modest shrine with a basilica of Constantinian type, in line with the other churches built in Rome in that period. Finished in 349 by Constantius, son of Constantine, the original San Pietro's was enriched throughout the centuries by donations and updatings by the popes and munificent princes. It was in Constantine's basilica that Charlemagne received the crown from the hands of Leo III in 800 and after him Lothair, Louis II, and Frederick III were crowned emperors. Even so, a thousand years after its foundation San Pietro's was falling into ruin and it was Nicholas V, on the advice of Leon Battista Alberti and with a plan by Bernardo Rossellino, who began to renovate and enlarge the Basilica. Various parts of the building were torn down, and work on the new tribune was started but soon came to a halt when Nicholas V died. Work was not resumed until 1506 when

Julius II della Rovere was pope. Most of the original church was dismantled by Bramante (who earned himself the title of « maestro ruiante »), with the intention of building ex novo a « modern » building in the classic style: a Greek-cross plan inspired by the Pantheon. Various supervisors succeeded each other until about the middle of the century: Fra Giocondo, Raphael, Giuliano da Sangallo, Baldassarre Peruzzi, Antonio da Sangallo the Younger, and, finally, Michelangelo, who needless to say interpreted Bramante's plan, modifying it in part, and envisioned the great dome (originally hemispherical) which crowned the renovated basilica. Michelangelo was succeeded by Vignola, Pirro Ligorio, Giacomo Della Porta, Domenico Fontana, all of whom interpreted his ideas quite faithfully. Then under Paul V, it was decided to reinstate the basilica plan, and return to the Latin-cross idea. With this in mind, the architect Carlo Maderno added three chapels to each side of the building and brought the nave as far as the present facade, the building of which was entrusted to him when he won an important competition. Work was begun in November of 1607 and terminated in 1612, after having « employed mountains of travertine from Tivoli ».
The **facade**, which is truly imposing in its proportions, is based on the use of the giant Corinthian order, which ar-

Above and right: the interior of San Pietro's with the Pope's High Altar and the Baldacchino, a masterpiece by Bernini. Left: the monument to John XXIII by Emilio Greco.

ticulates the front of the building with columns and pilasters. On the ground floor these frame a large central porch, with an arch on either side (the one on the left, the so-called Arch of the Bells, leads to Vatican City), and, above, a row of nine balconies. The crowning element is a canonic attic surmounted by a balustrade which supports thirteen enormous statues, representing all the *Apostles*, except for San Pietro, as well as Christ and St. John the Baptist. Above all looms **Michelangelo's imposing dome** with its strong ribbing, and, emerging from the front but to the side, the « minor » domes of the Gregoriana and the Clementina chapels by Giacomo Barozzi da Vignola. After the death of Carlo Maderno in 1629, the next director of works, Gian Lorenzo Bernini, left his unmistakeable mark. The prevalently Baroque character the building now displays was his doing. It is sufficient to mention the decorative transformation of the nave and the aisles, the erection of the justly famous bronze *baldacchino* (begun in 1624 and inaugurated on San Pietro's day in 1633), the decoration of the piers of the dome with four large statues, the installment at the back of the apse of the *Throne of San Pietro*, one of Bernini's most sumptuous inventions, a truly marvelous machine, built around the old wooden chair which a pious tradition says was used by the apostle Pietro. The organization of Piazza San Pietro, once more by Bernini, also dates to the papacy of Alexander VII (who financed the works for

The tomb of San Pietro.

Michelangelo's Pietà. ▶

the throne), while under Clement X the architect designed and built the small round temple which comprises the shrine of the Chapel of the Sacrament.

There are any number of chapels, all splendid in one way or the other, set along the perimeter of San Pietro's basilica, to begin with the **Chapel of the Pietà**, named after Michelangelo's famous marble sculpture of the *Pietà* which the young artist made between 1499 and 1500 for cardinal Jean de Bilheres. After the **Chapel of Saint Sebastian** (which contains Francesco Messina's *Monument to Pope Pius XII*) is the better known **Chapel of the Holy Sacrament** with Bernini's *ciborium* mentioned above and the bronze railing designed by Borromini; next is the **Gregoriana Chapel**, a late 16th-century work finished by Giacomo Della Porta and heavily decorated with *mosaics* and precious marbles; the **Chapel of the Column** with the astounding marble altarpiece depicting the *Encounter between St. Leo and Attila* by Algardi, and with the *sepulchers* of the many popes named Leo — the II, III, IV, XII; the **Clementina Chapel**, named after Pope Clement VII, built for him by Giacomo Della Porta, which houses the mortal remains of St. Gregory the Great; and, also by Della Porta, the sumptuous **Chapel of the Choir** decorated with gilded stuccoes; finally the **Chapel of the Presentation** with the recent *Monument to Pope John XXIII*, by Emilio Greco.

The Basilica of San Pietro in Vatican also contains a whole collection of famous monuments, from Michelangelo's *Pietà* to the venerated *effigy of San Pietro* shown in the act of blessing, which dates to the 13th century; Bernini's *Funeral Monument for Pope Urban VIII*, and the analogous *Funeral Complex for Paul III* by Guglielmo Della Porta, the *bronze Tomb* created by Antonio Pollaiolo for Pope Innocent VIII, which was part of the original San Pietro, and the neoclassic *Monument to the Stuarts* by Canova. Brief mention must also be made of the *baptismal font*, in porphyry, once part of a classical sarcophagus (and then used as the sepulcher for Otho II), transformed into a baptismal font by Carlo Fontana.

The imposing **Sacristy** lies before the left transept. Large as a church, it was conceived of as an independent building, and consists of the **Sagrestia Comune** on an octagonal central plan, the so-called **Sacristy of the Canons**, and the **Chapter Hall**. It was all designed by the Roman Carlo Marchionni at the behest of Pius VI, who laid the first stone in 1776.

Annexed to the Basilica is the **Museo della Fabbrica di San Pietro**, or Historical Artistic Museum, which includes the *Treasury of San Pietro's*. It was designed by Giovan Battista Giovenale and contains the remains of the enormous patrimony of the church which was repeatedly scattered and carried off by the Saracens, the Sack of Rome in 1527, the Napoleonic confiscations.

◄ Above: Michelangelo's imposing dome and, below, the interior showing the drum with the window's set between coupled pilaster strips, the ribs and the skylight in the lantern.

Panorama of the Vatican Palaces and the Vatican Museums.

VATICAN PALACES

One of the most sumptuous and articulated monumental complexes in the world is without doubt that of the Vatican Palaces, which began to be built in the 14th century so as to house as befitted their rank the popes who had finally « returned » from their stay in Avignon, and who had previously resided in the Lateran. The first pope to take up permanent abode in the Vatican was Gregory XI and his successors later enlarged and beautified the complex. In 1410 Alexander V had the communication « corridor » built between the palace and Castel Sant'Angelo. But the greatest impetus to the building and organization of the sumptuous complex was provided by Nicholas V. The heart of the complex is the square palace which encloses the famous **Cortile del Pappagallo**, and on which Leon Battista Alberti

and Bernardo Rossellino as well as others worked. The **Chapel of Nicholas V** is dedicated to Saints Stephen and Laurence and is decorated with *frescoes* by Fra Angelico. The world-famous **Sistine Chapel** was created between 1473 and 1480, under Sixtus IV, when Giovanni de' Dolci reconstructed what was originally the Palatine Chapel. Innocent VIII even went so far as to have himself a Palazzetto built on the highest point of the Belvedere. The building appears in Andrea Mantegna's paintings, but was then lost with Bramante's reorganization and a still later construction of the Museo Pio Clementino under Pope Pius VI. When Alexander VI once more took up residence in the square **Palace of Nicholas V**, his enlargement was terminated by the erection of the **Borgia Tower** (named after the pope's family).

The maecenas pope, Julius II, sponsored a reorganization

The Vatican Museums. Above: the Courtyard of the Fir Cone (Cortile della Pigna) with Bramante's niche. Below: the interior of the Gallery of Maps (Galleria delle Carte Geografiche).

Other rooms in the Vatican Museums with, below, left, ► one of the rooms in the Vatican Library (Biblioteca Apostolica).

Two masterpieces in the Museo Pio-Clementino: the Apollo Belvedere in the Octagonal Courtyard and Laocoön and his Sons.

The Biga (two-horsed chariot) from the Museo Chiaramonti ▶ recomposed by F.A. Franzoni (1788) from ancient fragments.

Following pages: four famous frescoes in Raphael's Stanze. Left, above: the Disputa or Disputation on the Holy Sacrament, in the Stanza della Segnatura; below: the School of Athens, in the same room. Right, above: the Expulsion of Heliodorus from the Temple, in the Stanza di Eliodoro; and, below, the Fire in the Borgo in the Stanza dell'Incendio nel Borgo.

which could fall under the heading of town planning when he entrusted Bramante with finding the solution of how to connect the Palace of Nicholas V with that of Innocent VII: the result was, as is known, the **Courtyard of the Belvedere** with the *niche* by Pirro Ligorio (1560) at one end, in turn derived from the transformation of Bramante's exedra with its twin flight of stairs. Bramante was also responsible for the elevation of the **Loggias of the Courtyard of Saint Damasus**, finished and decorated with frescoes by Raphael. Thanks to this expansion, the Pope's Palace could now face out on Piazza San Pietro. Between 1509 and 1512 Michelangelo frescoed the vault of the Sistine Chapel for Julius II, and in 1508 Raphael began to decorate the Stanze, which were finished in 1524. After the disastrous sack of Rome, which to some extent brought the grand papal project of the *Instauratio Urbis* to a halt, work on the Vatican Palace continued under Paul III, who entrusted Antonio da Sangallo the Younger with the building of the **Cappella Paolina**, the **Sala Ducale**, and the **Sala Regia**, entrusting the decoration of the Cappella Paolina and the termination of the frescoes in the Sistine to Michelangelo. The highlight of the Baroque in the Vatican Palace coincides with the papacy of Sixtus V and the architect Domenico Fontana, who designed the present papal residence and « cut » the Belvedere with the **Cortile trasversale** (now seat of the **Sistine Hall** of the Library).
In the 17th century, Urban VIII had the **Scala Regia** begun on designs by Bernini, as well as the **Pauline Rooms** in the Library and the Archives. In the following century the transformation into museums of part of the great complex was begun: the **Christian Museum (Museo Sacro)** and the **Profane Museum (Museo Profano)** (connected to the **Library**) were joined by the **Pio-Clementine Museum**, planned and installed by Michelangelo Simonetti and Giuseppe Camporese (1739-1771); by the **Chiaramonti Sculpture Gallery** bound to the name of Antonio Canova (1806-1810); the so-called **Braccio Nuovo** or **New Wing** designed by Raffaele Stern for Pius VII. Lastly, in the 20th century, Pope Pius XII initiated archaeological excavations under the Basilica of St. Peter's, while John XXIII turned his attention to the construction of new rooms which could better house the museum collections of the Lateran Palace.

RAPHAEL'S STANZE

The rooms known as Raphael's Stanze because they contain so many of the painter's masterpieces, were built under the papacy of Nicholas V. Their decoration was initially entrusted to Andrea del Castagno, Benedetto Bonfigli and Piero della Francesca. Afterwards, under Julius II, the undertaking passed to Lorenzo Lotto, Perugino, Sodoma, Baldassarre Peruzzi, and Bramantino. Only in the last phase, upon Bramante's advice, did Julius call in Raphael, who was already famous. The painter was also flanked by a choice team of « advisors ». Chronologically the first Stanza to be frescoed, or rather the vault, was the **Stanza della Segnatura**, so-called because this was where the court of the Segnatura met. Here Raphael painted the *Disputa* or *Disputation on the Sacrament*, which was thus his first pictorial work in Rome and which depicts the exaltation of the glory of the Eucharist rather than a « dispute ». Even more famous is the fresco on the wall across from the Disputa, the so-called *School of Athens*, which gathers the wise men and philosophers of antiquity together with the « contemporary » artists and lords, in other words the protagonists of the Renaissance, in an imposing architectural setting where they are all assembled around the great ancients, Plato and Aristotle. The composition of *Parnassus*, which decorates the wall of the window overlooking the Belvedere, is dated 1511 (the year is on the lintel of the window). The vault of the same Stanza has medallions which contain symbolic representations of *Philosophy, Justice, Poetry, Theology*, and panels with the *Fall of Man, The Judgement of Solomon, Apollo and Marsyas, Astronomy*.

Next, chronologically speaking, is the **Stanza di Eliodoro**, which furnishes an example of what might be called historical painting, for Raphael had proposed various miraculous events which were decisive in the story of the Church, perhaps suggested by Julius II. These included *Leo I repulsing Attila*, the *Mass of Bolsena*, the *Expulsion of Heliodorus*, the *Liberation of San Pietro*. These date to the years 1512-1514, while the vault was presumably frescoed by De Marcillat, who most likely continued Raphael's ideas. The decoration of the **Stanza dell'Incendio** however dates to 1514-1517. The name derives from the leading fresco which depicts the event of 847 when the *Fire in the Borgo* was miraculously stopped when Leo IV made the sign of the cross. An interesting detail in the fresco shows us the main facade of old San Pietro's, which had not yet been torn down when the picture was painted.

The last of the Stanze is the **Sala di Costantino**, which cannot really be said to be by Raphael for the work was carried out almost entirely by Giulio Romano after the Master's death, although the plans were certainly his. It was finished · in 1525. The decoration depicts episodes — famous and less famous — in the life of the emperor Constantine: from the *Baptism* (on the entrance wall), to the *Battle against Maxentius* (on the facing wall), the *Apparition of the Cross*, the mythical *Donation*. Raffaellino Del Colle and, above all, Francesco Penni were Giulio Romano's collaborators.

100

An allover view of the Sistine Chapel with Michelangelo's frescoes (the vault and the back wall with the Last Judgement), before restoration.

The Last Judgement. ▶

SISTINE CHAPEL

Between 1475 and 1481, under the pontificate of Sixtus IV Della Rovere, Giovannino de' Dolci, on a plan by Baccio Pontelli, built what may be called the Chapel of Chapels. Architecturally the Sistine Chapel is a spacious rectangular hall with a barrel vault, divided into two unequal parts by a splendid marble *transenna* or screen by Mino da Fiesole together with Giovanni il Dalmata and Andrea Bregno. The same artists also made the *choir loft*.

But the chief attractions of the Sistine Chapel are of course its frescoes, particularly those by Michelangelo, on the walls and vault. Michelangelo's marvelous paintings, however, came after others, which had been painted under the pontificate of Sixtus IV between 1481 and 1483, and which cover the wall facing the altar and the two side walls (these include paintings by Perugino, Pinturicchio, Luca Signorelli, Cosimo Rosselli, Domenico Ghirlandaio, Botticelli). The vault was blue and scattered with stars until Julius II commissioned Michelangelo to redecorate the vast surface.

Michelangelo worked on the ceiling from 1508 to 1512 and created a powerful architectural framework for the well-known figures of the *Sibyls* and the *Prophets*, the elegant bold *Ignudi*, the nine *Stories from Genesis*, including the universally famous *Creation of Man*.

Twenty-five years later, between 1536 and 1541, Michelangelo returned to the Sistine Chapel, this time under the papacy of Paul III Farnese. The new great fresco of the *Last Judgement* covers the whole back wall of the Sistine Chapel and it was so large that two of Perugino's frescoes had to be destroyed and two large arched windows had to be walled up.

MICHELANGELO IN THE SISTINE CHAPEL

Michelangelo, the famed master of the Sistine Chapel, completed his frescoes in two phases: the period between 1508 and 1512 was employed in painting the vaults under commission of Pope Julius II, whereas his other masterpiece, the Last Judgement, was commissioned by Pope Clement VII for the back wall of the chapel nearly a quarter of a century later. These two frescoes, which cover a surface of approximately 800 square meters, represent perhaps the greatest artistic achievement of all time. Beginning from the back, on the left-hand, side of the vault we can see: Jeremiah in meditation, the Persian Sibyl reading, Ezekiel holding a papyrus as he listens to an angel, the Eritrean Sibyl consulting a book, Joel reading a papyrus, Zachariah consulting a book, the Delphic Sibyl unwinding a papyrus, Isaiah in meditation with a book in his hand, the Cumaean Sibyl opening a book, Daniel writing, the Libyan Sibyl turning to pick up a book and last Jonah in ecstasy at the moment of his exit from the whale's belly. Above these twelve figures, softly rendered nude figures support festoons and medallions. In the center, nine pictures reproduce the stories of the Genesis: beginning from the one above the altar we find: God separating light from darkness, God creating the Sun, the Moon, and the plants on Earth, God separating the waters and creating fish and birds, followed by the well-known Creation of Adam, the Creation of Eve from Adam's rib, the Original sin and the Expulsion of Adam and Eve from the garden of Eden, the Flood, and Noah's drunkenness. The vault is also crowned by numerous triangular sections depicting other stories from the Old Testament: Judith and Holofernes, David and Goliath, Ahasuerus, Esther and Haman, and the Brazen serpent. The lunettes of the windows, and above them the vault sections, contain equally splendid frescoes depicting Christ's ancestors. An impressive pictorial composition representing the Last Judgement rotates around the commanding figure of Christ who, with an expressive and dramatic gesture, condems sinners.

THE RESTORED SISTINE CHAPEL

Thanks to the contribution of the Nippon Television Network Corporation and to its use of advanced technology, every detail in the restoration of the great Sistine Chapel frescoes by Michelangelo has been recorded. The restored frescoes have themselves caused considerable surprise among scholars and to some extent brought about a reconsideration of existing literature regarding the masterpieces. Whereas until recently Michelangelo was referred to as a painter of somber palette at the service of introspective chromatic research, during restoration the original colors, derkened by candle smoke, atmospheric conditions and still other causes, returned to their natural luminosity revealing light, emphatic tones of an unexpectedly « modern » coloristic effect, even as compared to his previous works. A rediscovered Michelangelo then — that of the Sistine Chapel — an artist who continues to astonish us after almost five centuries. The accompanying photographs reveal how difficult the work of restoration was. We can imagine the uncomfortable conditions under which Michelangelo was constrained to work, in a position requiring physical as well as creative and intellectual effort. The photographs on these pages show us the original restored colors used by Michelangelo in painting the Sibyls and the Prophets.

◄ A partial view of the Sistine Chapel.

A phase in restoration work and, at the side, a detail of a restored lunette.

On the following pages: a lunette of a window in the Sistine Chapel and the Creation of Adam. Insert: the Original Sin, the Expulsion from Paradise, and a detail of a lunette.

Above: a detail of a lunette after restoration. After the Sistine Chapel, Pope Julius II commissioned his tomb from Michelangelo, to be set up in the Basilica of San Pietro in Vincoli. Michelangelo's Moses (right), inspired by one of the greatest biblical figures, displays the same expressive intensity.

The entrance to the Basilica of San Pietro in Vincoli.
Below: the chains which are said to have bound the
apostle Peter.

BASILICA OF SAN PIETRO IN VINCOLI

This basilica stands on the slope of the Esquiline hill, over-looking the plain where the Capitoline, Palatine, and Cae-lian hills run together. The name of the church derives from a legend about Eudocia, wife of the emperor of the Eastern Empire, Theodosius II. During a pilgrimage to Jerusalem, she is said to have found the chains which had been used to bind the apostle Pietro. Part of these chains remained in Constantinople, but some of the links were sent to Rome to Eudocia minore who in turn presented them to the pope. And then came the miracle. While Leo the Great was hold-ing them, the links were miraculously welded together with other links said to come from the same holy chain and already venerated in Rome. Be that as it may San Pietro does not appear to have been consecrated by Leo the Great but by his predecessor, Sixtus III, who was pope from 432 to 440. Moreover the present building, the one which was consecrated, was preceded by another church of a different name. Excavations have revealed the remains of an apsed hall with a single nave and a « pierced » presbytery, dating to the third century and enclosed in the area of the church

Michelangelo's Moses between Rachel and Leah.

built in the middle of the 5th century by Philip, who however tended to a « modern » solution, replacing the simple straight hall with a tripartite structure with a transept. Perhaps the best known and most incisive restorations of the Basilica are the so-called Roverian restorations, promulgated by Cardinal Francesco Della Rovere (later Pope Sixtus IV) and above all Cardinal Giuliano Della Rovere, who became titular of St. Pietro in Vincoli in December 1471. These restorations, which were finished in 1475 (for the Jubilee) or at the latest in 1483, seem to have been planned and directed by the architect Baccio Pontelli, who appears also to have prepared the project for the renovation of the palace annexed to the Basilica and the adjoining Cloister, which were however not finished until Julius II. The *tomb of Julius II* was set up around 1540 after numberless vicissitudes. The contract that Michelangelo signed with the executors of the Pope's will is dated May 6, 1513, and stipulated for twenty-eight figures and three reliefs, all to be set in a suitable architectural setting. The entire project was to be finished in seven years at a total cost of 16,500 gold ducats. But as time went by, the project kept shrinking and the successive stages of the project are witnessed by contracts of 1516 and 1532. Ultimately the final

agreement between the artist and the heirs provided for only three statues by Michelangelo and three by Raffaello da Montelupo. All that now remains in San Pietro in Vincoli is the famous Moses, seated between *Rachel* (or the *Contemplative Life*) and *Leah* (or the *Active Life*), while the mortal remains of Julius II were wretchedly lost during the ill-omened sack of Rome in 1527. In the second half of the 16th century, still further modifications were carried out on the old Early Christian Basilica which had already been so heavily restored. An additional structure was added above the portico, which ended up by concealing the old openings so that new ones had to be put in. In 1705 Francesco Fontana, son of Carlo, was charged by Giovan Battista Pamphili with the screening off of the open trussed timber beams of the roof by means of a large wooden vault, while the framing of the portal on the interior by an aedicule dates to sixty years later. This was also when the Basilica was repaved in brick, altering the original level by raising the floor about ten centimeters. The last change was made by Vespignani and is mentioned here because it is an important element in the present aspect of the church. Vespignani worked on the area of the presbytery and replaced the Baroque altar with a typical open *ciborium* preceded by the confessio.

The Basilica of Santa Maria Maggiore.

Above, the mosaics in the conch of the apse and, below, the ▶
imposing interior of the basilica.

BASILICA OF SANTA MARIA MAGGIORE

In the 4th century a church, which was the ancestor of the present Basilica, was built on the hill of the Esquiline. The church was popularly called Santa Maria della Neve because Pope Liberius had drawn the perimeter in the snow which had miraculously fallen in the summer of 352. The present Church of Santa Maria Maggiore was completely rebuilt by Sixtus III (432-440) after the Council of Ephesus (and the holy arch does indeed bear the dedicatory inscription « XYSTUS.EPISCOPUS. PLE-BI. DEI »). The Basilica stayed as it was up to the 13th century when Eugene III had a portico built for the principal elevation, much like those still extant for example in San Lorenzo fuori le Mura or in San Giorgio al Velabro. At the end of that century, Nicholas IV promoted the renovation of the apse and not until the 18th century, after having demolished the original portico, did Benedict XIV entrust the creation of a new facade to Ferdinando Fuga.

This **facade** almost seems to be squeezed between two tall palaces (dating to the 17th and 18th centuries), and sits at the top of a spacious flight of steps. There is a portico with an architrave on the ground floor and a loggia with arches above, the whole crowned by a balustrade which curiously extends on either side of the facade to include the twin palaces at the sides. A rich sculptural decoration runs along the front and under the portico, while the loggia of the upper floor still preserves the mosaic decoration of the old 13th-century facade.

The **interior** is on a tripartite basilican plan with forty Ionic columns supporting a trabeation with a mosaic frieze. The flat *ceiling* is commonly attributed to Giuliano da Sangallo, while, as to be expected, the *pavement* is in Cosmatesque work although much of it was restored under Benedict XIV. An old tradition says that the rich gold decoration of the ceiling was made with the first gold that came from America, given to the Basilica by the Kings of Spain who were the illustrious protectors.

The chapels that branch off from the aisles mostly date to the 16th century. Of particular note are the **Sistine Chapel**, a Greek-cross plan with a cupola, by Domenico Fontana, and the **Paolina Chapel**, like the former in plan, by Flaminio Ponzio. Lastly, of importance in the right aisle is the Baptistery, also designed by Flaminio Ponzio, into which Valadier set a porphyry *baptismal font*.

119

CHURCH OF SANTA CROCE IN GERUSALEMME

According to tradition the church was built by St. Helena, Constantine's mother, and the composite name dates to after the 4th century, when the name of *Sancta Hierusalem* was joined to that of Santa Croce. It was here that the pope, during a fascinating ritual, showed the worshippers the golden rose, a symbol of the delights reserved for them in the perennial garden of the mystical celestial Jerusalem.

The animated facade which at present characterizes the **exterior** of Santa Croce, a play of concavities and convexities articulated by a tier of Corinthian pilasters, concludes in the center in a large curvilinear tympanum with the papal insignia. Further above, a fastigium, inserted into the attic and also suitably animated, supports the six *statues of Saints Helena, Luke, Matthew, John the Evangelist and Constantine*. The Romanesque **campanile** erected in 1144 under Lucius II contrasts with this impressive facade.

In the **interior** (thanks to the radical restoration it was subjected to in the course of the centuries) the only original elements remaining are the ground plan, part of the vertical structures (for example only eight of the twelve columns which once articulated the nave are left) and the fine Cosmatesque pavement. The decoration (including the architectural furnishings) is chronologically and stylistically bound to the various phases in the work that was continuously in progress in the building: mention can be made of the large *Triumph of the Cross* which decorates the already ornate ceiling and which is by Corrado Giaquinto da Molfetta, a pupil of Sebastiano Conca. Particularly effective is the fresco which covers the vault in the apse, depicting *Scenes of the Terrestral Jerusalem*: they were commissioned by Cardinal Carvajalo.

CHURCH OF SANTA MARIA SOPRA MINERVA

Built in the 8th century on the ruins of the temple of Minerva Calcidica it was rebuilt in 1280 in Gothic style and remains the only true example of Gothic architecture in Rome. In the course of the centuries it was often mercilessly remodelled and restored, culminating in the restoration of the 19th century which disfigured the purity of the inner facade and partially obliterated the original Gothic feeling. The 17th-century **facade** is simple but rather commonplace.

The imposing **interior** with its numerous chapels consists of a spacious nave.

The facade of the church of S. Croce in Gerusalemme (left) and that of Santa Maria sopra Minerva.

The facade of the Basilica of San Giovanni in Laterano.

Following pages: the interior with its Gothic tabernacle.

BASILICA OF SAN GIOVANNI IN LATERANO

Built by Constantine, plundered by the Vandals of Genseric, frequently sacked, damaged by the earthquake of 896 and various fires, the Basilica of San Giovanni in Laterano was continuously being rebuilt and restored, with the participation of Giovanni di Stefano, of Francesco Borromini, who brought it up to date for Innocent X, and Alessandro Galilei, who redid the facade in 1735. **Outside**, the Cathedral of Rome is characterized by the monumental architectonic structure of the giant Corinthian order used by Galilei, and it is enlivened by the jutting central part and the balustrade, above the attic, and the colossal statues of *Christ, Saints John the Baptist* and *John the Evangelist* and the *Doctors of the Church*. There are five entrances (the last to the right is known as « Porta Santa » and is opened only for the Holy Year or jubilee), surmounted by five loggias.

The imposing **interior** is a Latin cross with a nave and two aisles on either side. The antique columns were encased in robust piers, while grooved pilasters support a rich trabeation and above, a sumptuous ceiling, said to have been designed by Pirro Ligorio. Along the walls are ranged the figures of *Prophets, Saints,* and *Apostles* designed by Borromini but executed by his followers in the 18th century. At the crossing, the visitor unexpectedly finds himself at the Gothic heart of the Basilica: the *tabernacle* by Giovanni di Stefano, an airy slender silhouette against the gilded grates which enclose the precious relics of the heads of Saints Peter and Paul. Another of St. Peter's relics, the rough wooden altar table on which the apostle is said to have celebrated mass in the catacombs, is preserved in the papal altar. A double flight of stairs leads to the subterranean burial of Martin V, with its well-known *tomb slab* by Simone Ghini, probably under Donatello's supervision. The great conch of the apse at the back of the Basilica is covered with mosaics which date to different periods. Some are 4th cen-

121

tury, some 6th and some 13th century (note in particular the figures of the *Apostles*, signed by Jacopo Torriti). Above the organ, the large 19th-century frescoes by Francesco Grandi depicting episodes, both ancient and modern, concerning the *Founding and construction of the Basilica*. The decoration which entirely covers the transept also deals with this subject (including the *Conversion of Constantine*) and was completely restored under the papacy of Clement VIII by the architect Giacomo Della Porta and the painter known as Cavalier d'Arpino. Right under Cavalier d'Arpino's fresco of the *Ascension of Christ* is the *gable* in gilded bronze and supported by antique bronze columns which protects the *Altar of the Sacrament*, designed for Clement VIII by Pietro Paolo Olivieri and holding a precious *ciborium* like a small classic temple.

Among the chapels which were built in various periods as further decoration for the Basilica, note should be taken of the so-called **Cappella del Coro**, by Girolamo Rainaldi (1570-1655); the **Cappella del Crocifisso**, which preserves a fragment of the presumed *Funeral Monument of Nicholas IV*, attributed to Adeodato di Cosma (13th century); the **Cappella Massimo**, by Giacomo Della Porta; the **Cappella Torlonia**, unlike the precedent, splendidly in neo-Reinassance style by the architect Raimondi (1850); the **Cappella Corsini**, architecturally completely self sufficient, on a Greek-cross plan, by Alessandro Galilei for Clement XII. A corridor leads to the **Old Sacristy**, with the *Annunciation* by Venusti, and a *St. John the Evangelist* by Cavalier d'Arpino, and to the **New Sacristy**, with the 15th-century *Annunciation* of Tuscan school.

The Sanctuary of the Scala Santa.

The Scala Santa.

SCALA SANTA

The **Sanctuary** owes its name to the fact that it was originally built to contain, or incorporate, the **Pope's Chapel** or *Sancta Sanctorum*. Pope Sixtus V commissioned the palace from the architect Domenico Fontana in 1585-1590. The Chapel was originally part of a building known as »Patriarchio « (7th-8th century), when it housed the papal court.

The name **Scala Santa** derives from an erroneous identification of one of the staircases of the Patriarchio with a flight of stairs that was part of Pilate's *Praetorium* and which therefore would have been ascended by Christ when he was judged by Pilate. Nowadays the *Sancta Sanctorum* is used to indicate the **Chapel of Saint Laurence**, overflowing with relics and at the same time a true jewel of Cosmatesque art.

BASILICA OF SAN PAOLO FUORI LE MURA

Built by Constantine on the tomb of the apostle Paul, the church remained standing until July 15, 1823, when it was gutted by fire, not to be reconsecrated until 1854. On the **exterior**, St. Paul's now has an imposing quadriporticus in front of the main facade (on the side towards the Tiber) with 146 granite columns which define a space that is dominated by the statue of the *Apostle Paul*, by Pietro Canonica. The facade, which rises over the quadriporticus is richly decorated with mosaics both in the gable (the *Blessing Christ between Saints Peter and Paul*) and in the frieze (an *Agnus Dei* on a hill that rises up symbolically between the two holy cities of Jerusalem and Bethlehem) and the four large *Symbols of the Prophets*, which alternate with the three windows of the facade. The **interior** is just as richly decorated and is divided into a nave with two aisles on either side, separated by eighty columns in granite from Baveno. A continuous frieze runs along the crossing and the aisles with *Portraits of the 263 popes successors of Saint Peter*. On the walls, Corinthian pilasters rhythmically alternate with large windows with alabaster panes (which replace those destroyed in the explosion of 1893). The coffered ceiling has large gilded panels which stand out against the white ground.

Left: the facade of San Paolo fuori le Mura and, below, the interior of the basilica.

Two imposing statues of *Saints Peter and Paul* overlook the raised transept with the sumptuous *triumphal arch*, called the *Arch of Galla Placidia*, which dates to the time of Leo the Great, framing the apse which was already decorated with mosaics in the 5th century. In the 13th century the mosaics were renewed by Honorius III, using Venetian craftsmen who were sent for the purpose to the pope by the doge of Venice. The mosaics depict a *Blessing Christ between Saints Peter, Paul, Andrew, and Luke*, while Honorius, significantly in much smaller proportions, kisses the foot of the Savior. The *Redeemer* is also set on the gold-ground mosaic in the triumphal arch, this time flanked by two *Adoring Angels* and the *Symbols of the Evangelists*, dominating the two rows of the *Elders of the Apocalypse* with the slightly off-center figures of *Saint Peter and Saint Paul* on either side on a blue ground. Objects housed in the Basilica include the *tabernacle* Arnolfo di Cambio made in 1285 in collaboration with a certain « Petro », identified by some as Pietro Cavallini, also thought to have executed the *mosaics* (of which only fragments remain) decorating the back side of the arch of triumph and which once adorned the exterior of the Basilica. Under the fine canopy of Arnolfo's tabernacle is the altar beneath which is the *tomb of Saint Paul* with the inevitable *fenestrella confessionis* (confessional window) through which can be seen the epigraph incised on the stone « *Paulo Apostolo Mart.* », dating to the 4th century.

Two sections of the elegant cloister of San Paolo fuori le Mura.

The Basilica of San Lorenzo fuori le Mura.

Above: the facade of Santa Maria in Trastevere and, below, ►
the interior of the church.

BASILICA OF SAN LORENZO FUORI LE MURA

Built on the tomb of the deacon Laurence during Constantinian's time, the basilica was enlarged in 1210 and between 1848 and 1864. The main **facade** is now preceded by a hexastyle narthex on antique columns (the capitals are of more recent date) which support a simple trabeation with mosaic decoration, while the **interior** of the portico repeats the decoration of a feigned curtain wall in red and white. Three entrances lead into the **interior** which is characterized by an evident lack of homogeneity: a typical basilica with a nave and two aisles, ending in a triumphal arch (the *Honorian Basilica*, known also as « western ») and a second lower structure, not in line with the former, with columns on three sides and a women's gallery (which is the Pelagian Basilica, known also as « eastern »). The « eastern » Basilica also contains the *Tomb of St. Laurence* in the nave, in correspondence to the ciborium (dated 1148) by the Roman marble artisans Giovanni, Pietro, Angelo, and Sasso, sons of Paolo. Lastly the Pelagian mosaic on the central arch depicts the *Blessing Christ* with an astylar cross, *between Saints Peter, Paul, Laurence and Stephen*, and at either end, *Hippolitus* and *Pelagius II*, who as to be expected offers the Saviour a model of the renewed church.

CHURCH OF SANTA MARIA IN TRASTEVERE

Founded as early as the 3rd century by Saint Calixtus and terminated under St. Julius, Santa Maria in Trastevere basically maintained its original aspect, notwithstanding various restorations in the course of the centuries (as was the case with other churches of more or less this period), until the 18th century, when Pope Clement XI had the architect Carlo Fontana add on a portico.

The **facade** therefore has a large crowning gable, and is divided by three large arched openings which correspond to the three richly decorated portals under the portico.

The **interior** is, as to be expected, a tripartite basilica with columns of various diameters and orders (Ionic and Corinthian), with a presbytery, and an apse that is decorated with *mosaics* by Pietro Cavallini as well as other mosaics (in the upper zone) that date to the middle of the 12th century. Various chapels are scattered along the perimeter of the church, the most outstanding of which (due also to their position on either side of the apse) are the so-called **Winter Choir** and the richly decorated **Altemps Chapel** by Martino Longhi the Elder. Lastly, next to the Basilica is the fine Romanesque **campanile** which has an ancient bell over the roof.

CHURCH OF SANTA MARIA IN COSMEDIN

In the 6th century the Church of Santa Maria in Cosmedin was built near the temples of Hercules and of Ceres on the remains of a large porticoed hall dating to the Flavian period. The name derives from the Greek, for it had been turned over to Greeks who had escaped the iconoclastic persecution and who probably decorated it (the word « Cosmedin » could refer to these « ornaments »). The *Schola Graeca*, as the church was also called, was then restored by Nicholas I, Gelasius II and Calixtus II, respectively, in the 9th and 12th centuries, when the women's galleries were walled up and lost, although the church acquired a new porch with a central vestibule. In the 18th century Giuseppe Sardi decorated the **facade** richly, but the restorations Giovenale carried out at the end of the 19th century restored the church to its original state, bringing it into line with the tall Romanesque **bell tower**. The **interior**, which had also frequently been remodelled in the course of the centuries, was also restored to the original 8th-century forms with a few concessions to the 12th-century style. What we have then is a typical basilican ground plan with a nave and two aisles, divided by piers and reused antique columns, and terminating in three apses. The **Chapel of the Choir** and the **Sacristy**, access to which is from the right aisle, were then added to the actual basilica. The architectural decoration, also strictly in keeping with the original style, includes the paschal candlestick, the bishop's cathedra, the baldachin over the high altar, the monolithic altar in red granite. The **crypt**, which consists of three rooms and a small apse, was obtained from the foundations of the Flavian hall. Only a part of all this is still original for most of what we see is the result of restoration.

◄ The facade of Santa Maria in Cosmedin.

Above: the interior of the church.
Below: the ''Bocca della Verità''.

ARCH OF JANUS

A large four-sided marble arch, which stands between the Velabrum and the Forum Boarium, can be identified with an *arcus divi Constantini* mentioned in the Regionaries of the Constantinian period, in Region XI. Fragments of the dedicatory inscription from the arch are walled in the facade and interior of the Church of S. Giorgio in Velabro and seem to indicate that it was erected in honor of Constantine, probably by Constantius II around A.D. 256 when he visited Rome.

The conventional name of Arch of Janus derives from the term *Ianus* (patron god of gateways) used to designate co-vered passegeways, arcades and arches.

It measures 12 meters per side and is 16 meters high. The four piers, faced with marble slabs (in part reused), stand on molded plinths. Above the plinth,, the two outer faces of each pier have two rows of semi-circular niches with shell-shaped conchas, which held statues and were separated by a cornice. Originally they must have been framed by small columns which in the lower row rested on the cornice of the plinth, and the upper row rested on the cornice at the height of the opening. The round arches lead into barrel vaults which at their crossing form a cross vault with brick ribbing. The attic, of brick faced with marble, was torn down in 1827 as a medieval addition. The predilec-

◄ The four-sided Arch of Janus, dating to Constantinian times.

The Church of San Giorgio in Velabro.

tion for a facade of niches framed by small columns on corbels is typical of the 4th century. The Arch of Janus therefore can be compared with the north apse of the Basilica of Maxentius, Maxentius' restructuration in 307 of the temple of Venus in Rome, with the facade of Diocletian's palace in Spalato and with the changes made by Diocletian inside the Curia.

CHURCH OF SAN GIORGIO IN VELABRO

The church of San Giorgio in Velabro stands behind the Arch of Janus. The name derives from the Velabrum, the marsh where Faustulus found Romulus and Remus. Probably dating to the 6th century, it was rebuilt by Leo II (682-83) and completely restored in 1926 when the Baroque superstructures and ornamentation were removed. To the left of the facade with its portico of Ionic columns and corner piers in brick, stands the robust Romanesque bell tower of the 12th century. Inside, the nave and aisles are separated by columns of marble and granite. Of note is the Cosmatesque tabernacle with two tiers of small columns.

133

The twin churches of Santa Maria di Loreto and of the Santissimo Nome di Maria.

Above: the sober facade of Santa Maria d'Aracoeli at the top of the flight of steps with, on the right, a view of the Capitoline Hill. Below: the interior of Santa Maria d'Aracoeli. ▶

CHURCHES OF SANTA MARIA DI LORETO AND SANTISSIMO NOME DI MARIA

These two churches, both on the Largo del Foro Traiano, have the same central plan although the former, dedicated to the **Madonna of Loreto**, was founded at the beginning of the 16th century (1501) while the latter was built between 1736 and 1738 after plans by Antonio Derizet. The plans for the robust square building block and the cupola which rises up over it, as well as the corresponding octagon in the interior, to be found in Santa Maria di Loreto, have been attributed to artists as prestigious as Bramante and Antonio da Sangallo the Younger.

Despite their external resemblance, the interior of the **Church of the Santissimo Nome di Maria** is on an elliptical plan with seven sumptuous chapels opening off the perimeter.

CHURCH OF SANTA MARIA D'ARACOELI

Mention of the church appears as early as the 7th century. In the 10th century it became a Benedictine Abbey and then passed to the Friars Minor, who saw to its reconstruction around 1320. A place for associative life as well as a place of worship, the church continued in this unique calling into the 16th century and the civic victory of Marcantonio Colonna after the victory of Lepanto (1571) was celebrated here. The **exterior** has a gabled roof and three doorways under three windows. A sort of vestibule is set against the central portal. Renaissance elements of some importance in the austere 14th-century facade are the reliefs with *Saints Matthew and John* over the two smaller portals. The **interior**, a typical basilica, has a nave separated from the two side aisles by 22 reused antique columns. The *Cappella Bufalini* (in the right aisle) contains frescoes by Pinturicchio that are considered his masterpieces.

134

BAROQUE AND MONUMENTAL ROME

*I*n the Renaissance and above all in the 17th and 18th centuries Rome was in constant flux, structurally and artistically, in the attempt to adapt its appearance to its increasingly evident role of official representative of the Universal Church and center of diffusion for the Catholic religion and culture, as well as capital of the temporal dominion of the popes. In their hopes of transforming Rome into an inimitable city on a universal level and of passing into history as great patrons, many popes called artists from all over Italy to their courts. Painters, sculptors and architects worked with great zeal and abnegation at the tasks assigned, as exemplified by the afflictions and frustrations Michelangelo was subjected to at the beginning of the 16th century during the four years in which he frescoed the **Sistine Chapel** for Pope Julius II (1508-1512). A simple analysis of the dates relative to the foundation and the inauguration of so many of the churches, piazzas, palaces and villas, gardens and fountains makes one aware that in certain periods the entire city must have seemed like an immense construction yard, with scaffolding at every corner and teeming with laborers and artists at work. Actually much of Rome's present monumental and urbanistic layout, characterized above all by the great development of Baroque architecture, derives from the realization of the great projects of art and architecture that matured in this phase of the city's history. Many of these structures still stand out in the urban context of Rome. In part this also depends on the unstinting use of a building material which was ideally suited to the style and proportions of the civic and religious buildings of this period: travertine, a porous rock of chemical-organogenic origins that is light in color (and therefore ideal in stressing the play of lights and shadows in the decoration) and which is available **in loco** (the Parioli) or in any case within the confines of the Papal State (Tivoli, etc.).

The papal administration however was not alone in committing itself both financially and technically to this great task of restructuration: private citizens, in particular, of course, the upper social classes, did their part in beautifying Rome with a rich series of palaces, villas, gardens, etc. Moreover, as has been noted, the Roman aristocracy had already monopoli-

zed the office of pontiff, receiving in exchange economical benefits, juridical privileges, public offices, and real estate. From the 15th to the 18th centuries, in particular, the popes recurrently resorted to nepotism and lavished honor and riches on the members of their family, which obviously were paid for out of the State budget. It is no accident for example that the villas and palaces of the nobles were planned and built by the great families (Orsini, Colonna, Farnese, Borgia, Barberini, Pamphili, Chigi, Della Rovere, etc.) during the pontificate of one of their illustrious members.

Large buildings that were essentially for private use began to be built as early as the Renaissance. Examples are the **Villa of the Farnesina** (B. Peruzzi 1510), **Villa Madama** (Raphael 1516-1517), **Villa Giulia** (Vignola 1550-155), etc., or such as **Palazzo Venezia** (L.B. Alberti, P. and M. Barbo 1455-1464), **Palazzo della Cancelleria** (Bramante 1511), **Palazzo Farnese** (Antonio da Sangallo the Younger (1514-1540), **Palazzo Massimo** (B. Peruzzi 1532-1536), **Palazzo Caetani-Ruspoli** (B. Ammannati 1556), **Palazzo del Quirinale**, summer residence of the popes (F. Ponzio and O. Mascherino 1574-1740), etc. Inside these magnificent buildings the nobles installed real courts in miniature and in turn patronized the artists of the period, commissioning works of art with which to embellish their mansions. In addition to a newly discovered aesthetic taste, the construction of these great opulent buildings clearly mirrors the desire of the wealthy Roman patricians to use art as a means by which to vindicate and flaunt their privileged social «status», that clearly set them apart from the masses in the capital. These elegant structures, their mass only in part lightened and embellished by surface decoration, seem in fact to flout the crumbling unwholesome constructions of the lower classes. These splendid residences continued to be built throughout the 17th and 18th centuries and the city was enriched with an immense artistic and architectural patrimony without equal: **Villa Borghese** (G. Vasanzio 1613-1615), **Villa Ludovisi** (1621-1623) and **Villa Pamphili** (A. Algardi 1650), various palaces such as **Barberini** (C. Maderno, F. Borromini, G. Bernini

1625-1633), **Spada** (F. Borromini 1640), **Doria-Pamphili** (A. Valvassori 1734), **Corsini** (F. Fuga 1732-1736) and **Montecitorio** (G. Bernini and C. Fontana 1641-1694), etc. Monumental architecture for public use was also given substantial impetus in these two centuries with the layout of the **staircase of Trinità de' Monti** (A. Specchi and F. De Sanctis 1721-1725) and the creation of various fountains including the **Tritone** (G. Bernini 1632-1637), the **Janiculum**, of the **Acqua Paola** (F. Ponzio and G. Fontana 1612), of the **Barcaccia** (P. Bernini 1627-1629), **of the Rivers** (G. Bernini 1651), **of Trevi** (N. Salvi 1732), etc. The most important artists of this period are without doubt Francesco Castelli (Borromini) and Gian Lorenzo Bernini, who were active in the field of religious architecture as well as in civil structures. Bernini's artistic genius emerges above all in the definitive arrangement of the **Piazza** and the **Colonnade of St. Peter's** while Borromini distinguished himself in the **churches of S. Carlo alle 4 Fontane** (1638-1641), **S. Ivo alla Sapienza** (1642-1660) and **S. Agnese in Agone** (1653-1657). In the course of the 18th century the Papal State however began gradually to go into a political and economic decline. In foreign affairs the choice of a universalistic and paternalistic policy on the part of the Church and its consequent absolute neutrality within the national and social conflicts in Europe led in fact to its gradual subjection to the great European powers and an increasing isolation from the Italian vicissitudes which also extended to the field of culture. In domestic politics there was an absolute incapacity to take effective action in the face of the economic and social crisis that depended on the corruption and exorbitant venality of the papal administrators, the confusion in state finances bled by nepotism, and the intolerable malversation of the rich and powerful. Activity in the fields of art and architecture obviously reflected this new economic and social crisis: projects for new buildings, above all on a monumental scale, grew less frequent and less pretentious and energy was diverted into the renewal of existing works such as **S. John in Lateran** (A. Galilei 1734-1735), **S. Maria Maggiore** (F. Fuga 1743-1750), **S. Croce in Gerusalemme** (D. Gregorini and P. Passalacqua 1743) and **S. Maria degli Angeli** (L. Vanvitelli 1749). Initially at least the revolutionary tempest that arrived from France at the beginning of the 19th century introduced new ferments in art and town planning. Napoleon's desire to restore Rome to its original Imperial splendors, contemporaneously maintaining its subordination to Paris, opened the way to the diffusion of the neoclassic style and further monumental development. The best results of this small aesthetic revolution are to be found in the reorganization of the **Piazza del Popolo** and the **Pincio** by G. Valadier (1816-1820). When the pope's temporal power was restored, this new-found artistic ferment soon dried up and was infused with new life only when the Capital of Italy was transferred to Rome. The need to adapt the urban structure to the new bureaucratic and administrative exigencies, typical of a modern capital, made it necessary to construct new public buildings such as the **Ministry of Finance** near Porta Pia (R. Canevari 1877), the **Palace of Justice** (G. Calderini 1889-1910) and the **Policlinico**; road infrastructures, such as the twelve new bridges over the Tiber and the Corso Vittorio Emanuele, and celebrative and commemorative monuments such as the **monument to Victor Emmanuel II** (G. Sacconi 1888). In the name of recreating and safeguarding the aesthetic and iconographic aspect of the city, discutable projects for the «urban renewal» of the historical center were carried out, resulting in the destruction of large portions of the districts there. This policy was carried to an extreme during the Fascist period when the scenarios for the celebration of the glorious deeds of the regime were reconstructed. As was the case in the Rome of the Empire and in that of the overbearing and corrupt popes, under Fascism too the dominating classes utilized art as a demagogic means of power and political pressure on the masses. Buildings that fall into this category include the **Palazzo della Civiltà del Lavoro** (G. Guerrini, B. Lapadula and M. Romano), **dei Congressi** (A. Libera 1938) and the **Palazzo delle Tradizioni Popolari**; sport facilities, such as the **Foro Italico** (E. Del Debbio and L. Moretti), and the great thoroughfares for celebrative use, such as the **Via dei Fori Imperiali**. The new administrative, monumental and residential district of **EUR** (M. Piacentini 1938) and much of the construction of the **Stazione Termini** also date to this period.

Following pages: the staircase of the Campidoglio with the statues of the Dioscuri and the Palazzo Senatorio.

Piazza del Campidoglio, with Marcus Aurelius surrounded by the Palazzo dei Conservatori, Palazzo Senatorio and Palazzo Nuovo.

THE CAPITOLINE

From earliest times on, the Capitoline hill (or Campidoglio) was the center of the political, social, and religious life of Rome. In addition to the old *asylum*, this was the site of the great Italic temple dedicated to the Capitoline Jupiter, and the name of *Capitolium* was used almost exclusively to designate the temple rather than the entire site. Among others the *arx*, with the Temple of Iuno Moneta (the Admonisher) and the temple of the Virtus, also stood on the northern tip of the two knolls which comprised the height. The *clivus capitolinus* was the carriage road which led to the hill of the forum; there was also a flight of stairs which led to the arx alone and from which, near the Mamertine Prisons, the famous *Scalae Gemoniae* branched off.

The most sacred of the hills of Rome (even though the smallest) has continued to be the seat of power throughout the centuries. Michelangelo's **Piazza del Campidoglio** now stands on its summit, defined by illustrious palaces and magnificently decorated by the **statue of Marcus Aurelius**, set at the center of the intriguing interplay of elipses and volutes Michelangelo himself designed on the gray pavement of the square. Formerly in the Lateran square, the Marcus Aurelius was moved to the Capitoline in 1538 and had not apparently been previously taken into consideration by Michelangelo as decoration for the square.

The Palazzo Senatorio, the Palazzo Nuovo (or of the Capitoline Museum) and the Palazzo de'Conservatori define the limits of this first plateau of modern Rome. Both the **Palazzo Nuovo** and the **Palazzo dei Conservatori** were designed as twins by Michelangelo and built respectively by Girolamo Rainaldi (under Innocent X) and Giacomo Della Porta (after 1563). Both of Michelangelo's palaces are characterized by an architectural layout sustained by large Corinthian pilasters, and are crowned by an attic with a balustrade supporting large statues.

The **Palazzo Senatorio**, however, with a facade that is attributed to Rainaldi and Della Porta (although there was an earlier project by Michelangelo) stands on the historical site of the *Tabularium* and is distinguished by its converging flights of stairs, designed by Michelangelo and built while the artist was still alive. Inside is a series of fa-

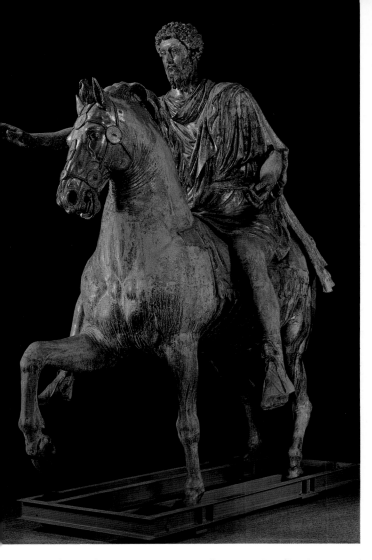

Above: the equestrian statue of Marcus Aurelius (at present inside the Palazzo Nuovo). Right, above: the statue of the seated Minerva, in the recess on the facade of the Palazzo Senatorio; below: detail of the figure of the Tiber, which together with the Nile, adorn the sides of the Palazzo Senatorio.

mous rooms, including the *Sala delle Bandiere*, that of the *Carroccio* (or *Chariot*), the *Green Room*, the *Yellow Room*, and the large *Council Hall* where the Senate Tribune met. The Palazzo Nuovo contains the **Capitoline Museum**, which is well known both for the wealth of material and for the fact that it is the oldest museum collection in the world. Begun by Sixtus IV, in 1471, it was enriched by popes Pius V, Clement XII (who opened it to the public), Benedict XIV, Clement XIII and Pius VI. Installed on two floors, the collection of the Capitoline Museum occupies practically all the rooms on the ground floor, as well as those on the upper floor, including the hall. Note should be taken on the first floor of the *Egyptian Collection* and, in the *Hall of Oriental Cults*, of an impressive series of statues, inscriptions, and reliefs. Treasures of classic art are contained in the other rooms on the ground floor (to the right of the atrium) and on the upper floor. In particular the monuments in the *Hall of Columns* and the *Hall of Emperors* (with *65 busts of Roman emperors*) come to mind as well as the *Hall of Philosophers*, the *Hall of the Faun*, and the famous *Hall of the Dying Gaul* (also called the *Dying Gladiator*).

Above: the facade of the Palazzo Nuovo, seat of the Capitoline Museums, designed by Michelangelo together with its twin, the Palazzo dei Conservatori. Below, right the 19th-century monument to Cola di Rienzo and, left, the wolf, symbol of Rome.

On the facing page, one of ▶ the Dioscuri flanking the staircase of the Piazza del Campidoglio.

The interior of the Mamertine Prisons.

PALAZZO VENEZIA

Outstanding monuments and historical buildings overlook the Piazza Venezia. The most important, on the west side of the square, is the **Palazzo Venezia**, the design for which is attributed to Leon Battista Alberti, while the actual building was carried out under Bernardo Rossellino. Commissioned by Pietro Barbo (future Pope Paul II) and terminated by Marco Barbo, Pietro's nephew, the building was the headquarters of the Venetian embassy in Rome, and, as Venetian territory, even belonged to the Austrians until 1916. More recently it was the representative seat of Mussolini's government and the dictator had his cabinet meetings here (in the *Sala del Mappamondo*). Ever since 1944 it has been the home of the Museum of Palazzo Venezia, a particularly privileged exhibition site. The main facade of the palace faces onto the Piazza Venezia and is distinguished by a tripartite architectural layout and large cross windows on the *piano nobile*. Of note on the doorway are the *Barbo coats of arms* and, on the facade on the Via del Plebiscito, the other *portal* decorated by Giovanni il Dalmata. Inside, on the other side of the atrium, is the *courtyard* partially defined by Giuliano da Maiano's incompleted *portico*.

Inside Palazzo Venezia, the **Museo di Palazzo Venezia** is installed in the rooms of *Paul II's Apartment* and in the adjacent *Cybo Apartment* (as well as in part of the *Palazzetto di Venezia*). Characterized by the variety of material on exhibition (in part due to the varied tastes of the popes-collector), the collections of Palazzo Venezia occupy a series of rooms: the *Sala Regia*, with the collections of arms and tapestries, the *Sala delle Battaglie* or *of the Concistoro*, the famous *Sala del Mappamondo*, the *Hall of the Labors of Hercules*, which contains wooden sculpture, and another six rooms full of fine collections of silver and ceramics.

MAMERTINE PRISONS

Under the Church of S. Giuseppe dei Falegnami, on the slopes of the Capitoline hill, north of the Temple of Concord, are the « prisons » known in medieval times as « Mamertine ». The travertine facade of the building can be dated from the inscription referring to the consuls Gaius Vibius Rufinus and Marcus Cocceius Nerva who were consuls between 39 and 42 A.D. A modern entrance leads into a trapezoidal chamber built in blocks of tufa, dating to the middle of the 2nd century B.C. A door which is now walled up led into the other rooms of the prison called « *latomie* » because they were adapted from the tufa quarries. A circular opening in the pavement of this room was originally the only entrance to an underground chamber where those condemned to death and enemies of the State were tortured and killed, generally by strangulation. It only appears to be a later legend that St. Peter was kept prisoner here.

MONUMENT TO VICTOR EMMANUEL II

After an extenuating competition, the realization of the monument was entrusted to Giuseppe Sacconi and was begun in 1885, to be finished and inaugurated in 1911. Its intentions were those of celebrating the splendor of the nation after the Unification of Italy, and with this in mind Sacconi envisioned it in imposing classicistic forms that would mirror the emotional and patriotic heart of the monument, the **Altar to the Homeland**, which was in turn envisioned as architecture within architecture with the solemn statue of *Rome* keeping watch over the **Tomb of the Unknown Soldier**. Note should also be taken of the **equestrian statue of Victor Emmanuel II**, for it is an integral part of the monument, also decidedly classicistic in style, as well as the fateful words from the Bulletin of Victory of Nov. 4, 1918.

PANTHEON

The first building was erected in 27 B.C. by Marcus Vipsanius Agrippa, the faithful advisor of Augustus.
In Trajan's time, the temple was completely rebuilt by Hadrian between 118 and 128, in the form we still see today. The inscription on the frieze of the porch, *M(arcus) Agrippa L(uci) f(ilius) co(n)s(ul) tertrium fecit*, was therefore placed there by Hadrian who never put his own name on any of the monuments he built.
Hadrian's reconstruction profoundly modified the original building. The facade was set facing north, the porch was set on the site occupied by the original temple and the large rotunda coincided with the open area in front. Still today the large columned porch has a facade composed of eight columns in grey granite. Two red granite columns each are set behind the first, third, sixth, and eighth column of the facade, thus forming three aisles. The central aisle, which is the widest, leads to the entrance. The side aisles end in two large niches destined for the statues of Agrippa and Augustus. The tympanum was decorated with a crowned eagle in bronze of which only the fix-holes still remain. The ceiling of the porch was also decorated in bronze but this was removed by Pope Urban VIII Barberini (which lies at the root of the famous pasquinade: « *quod non fecerunt barbari, fecerunt Barberini* »).
Behind the porch is a massive construction in brick, which joins it to the Rotonda, a gigantic cylinder with a wall that is six meters thick, divided into three superposed sectors, marked externally by cornices. The wall gets lighter as it rises, and the thickness of the walls, with brick vaulting in various places, is not always completely solid. The height of the Rotonda to the top of the dome is precisely that of its diameter (m. 43.30) so that the interior space is a perfect sphere. The dome is a masterpiece of engineering: it is the largest dome ever covered by masonry and it was cast in a single operation on an imposing wooden centering.
The interior of the building has six distyle niches at the sides and a semicircular exedra at the back, with eight small aedicules in between which have alternating arched and triangular pediments. The dome is decorated with five tiers of lacunar coffering except for a smooth band near the oculus, the circular opening (9 m. diam.) which illuminates the interior.

COLUMN OF MARCUS AURELIUS

Set at the center of Piazza Colonna, it was named after the emperor Marcus Aurelius, who had it erected between 189 and 196 in honor of his victories over the Marcomanni, the Quadi and the Sarmatians. Almost 30 meters high, the shaft is enveloped by a bas-relief spiral, which, like the one on Trajan's Column, narrates the events of the Germanic and Sarmatian wars. The statue of *Saint Paul* on the top was set there by Domenico Fontana in 1588 and replaced the one of Marcus Aurelius once there.

◄ Left, above: Piazza della Rotonda with Giacomo Della Porta's fountain with an Egyptian obelisk in the foreground and the Pantheon. Below: the interior of the Pantheon. The first two kings and the first queen of Italy are buried here in what is the most outstanding architectural monument of ancient Rome.

The Aurelian Column.

The site was originally in the heart of the imperial Rome of the Antonines, between the Temple of Marcus Aurelius and the Temple of Hadrian.

Now the column rises in Piazza Colonna with a base restored by Fontana who, as shown by the inscription, erroneously thought it had been dedicated to Antoninus Pius. The interior of the column is hollow and a spiral staircase of 190 steps leads to the top.

Two views of the Fontana di Trevi.

TREVI FOUNTAIN

It may or may not be the most beautiful fountain in Rome but it is without doubt the most famous. The imaginative concept, the theatrical composition, the sober and imposing beauty of the sculptured marble figures make it a true masterpiece both of sculpture and of architecture. Pietro da Cortona and above all Bernini, who began the undertaking, both had a hand in the project. The death of Pope Urban VIII brought work to a standstill and it was not until about a hundred years later that Clement XII entrusted the work to Nicola Salvi, who finished the undertaking between 1732 and 1751.

The fountain is highly symbolic with intellectual connotations. A tall and sober *Arch of Triumph* (the palace of Neptune) dominates the scene from on high. It is comprised of an order of four Corinthian columns and is surmounted by an attic with statues and a balustrade. A large niche at the center of the arch lends balance and symmetry to the

whole ensemble. A smaller niche to the left contains the statue of *Abundance* by F. Valle, and above this is a fine relief depicting *Agrippa approving the plans for the Aqueduct* by Andrea Bergondi. The niche on the right contains the figure of *Salubrity*, also by F. Valle, with a relief above of the *Virgin showing soldiers the Way*, by G. B. Grossi.

The central niche seems to impart movement to the imposing figure of *Neptune* who firmly guides a chariot drawn by sea horses, known as the « *agitated horse* » and the « *placid horse* », names obviously derived from the way in which the two animals have been represented. As they gallop over the water, the horses are guided in their course by fine figures of *tritons* which emerge from the water and which were sculptured by P. Bracci in 1762. The setting all around consists of rocks.

ELEPHANT OF PIAZZA DELLA MINERVA

Considered one of Bernini's most delightful inventions, the *elephant* serves as the support for the Egyptian *obelisk* dating to the 6th century B.C., formerly set up in the nearby Isaeum Campense or Temple of Isis. Sculptured by Ercole Ferrata in 1667, it is relatively so small that it is popularly known as « Minerva's chick », even though the inscription on the base transforms it into the symbol of a robust intellect capable of supporting great wisdom, by which the obelisk is meant.

Left, above: one of Neptune's horses in the Fontana di Trevi and, below, a Triton. Below: the elephant with the obelisk in Piazza della Minerva.

Above: Piazza del Popolo. Right: the water clock in the Pincio.

PIAZZA DEL POPOLO

Piazza del Popolo, one of the most characteristic areas of neoclassical Rome, is the child of Giuseppe Valadier's creative genius in the field of town planning and architecture, a project he began work on in 1793.

It is distinguished by the low exedras which define the boundaries of the square and which are topped by statues of the *Four Seasons*, while the center is emphasized by the two fountains, *Neptune and the Tritons* and *Rome between the Tiber and the Aniene River*. All the sculpture mentioned above dates to the first half of the 19th century and was made respectively by Gnaccarini, Laboureur, Stocchi, Baini, Ceccarini.

PINCIO

The public gardens of the Pincio stretch out on the slope beyond the exedra to the right of the Piazza del Popolo. Like the Piazza, they too were laid out by Giuseppe Valadier between 1810 and 1818. Already famous in antiquity, the site was occupied by the Gardens (*horti*) of Lucullus, the Acilia family, the Domizi, and finally the Pinci after whom the site, and then the park, was named. In line with a typically Italian type of garden architecture, *busts* of men famous in the world of art and history are scattered throughout the Pincio.

151

In this page: Castel Sant'Angelo. In the insert: a panorama of the
Tiber with the Ponte Sant'Angelo
and Castel Sant'Angelo.

Castel Sant'Angelo.

CASTEL SANT'ANGELO

Castel Sant'Angelo, whose imposing mass still dominates the panorama of Rome, and which is known as the *Mole Adriana*, was not originally built for defensive purposes but as the funeral monument of the emperors. A new bridge (called Pons Aelius from the *nomen* of the emperor) which still exists as **Ponte S. Angelo** was built to put the monument in communication with the Campus Martius. This bridge flanks Nero's bridge, further downstream. It consisted of three large central arches and two inclined ramps supported by three smaller arches on the right bank and two on the left bank.

Most of the structural parts of the Mausoleum, which was incorporated into Castel Sant'Angelo in the Middle Ages, have been preserved. The building consisted of an enormous quadrangular basement, 89 m. per side and 15 m. high. On top was a cylindrical drum (diam. 64 m., height 21 m.) flanked by radial walls. A tumulus of earth planted with trees rose up over the drum. Along the edges were decorative marble statues and at the center, raised even higher up, was a podium with columns on top of which was a bronze quadriga with the statue of Hadrian. The exterior of the enclosure was faced with Luna marble and with inscriptions of the *tituli* of the personages buried in the monument; engaged pilasters were set at the corners and the upper part was decorated with a frieze of garlands and bucrania (fragments are preserved in the Museo del Castello). The drum was faced on the outside with travertine and fluted pilaster strips. The entire monument was enclosed in a wall with bronze gates, decorated with peacocks (two are in the Vatican), perhaps a funerary symbol.

The original entrance to the tomb, with three openings, was on the side of the base that faces the river. The current entrance is at least three meters higher up. From here a corridor (*dromos*) led to a square vestibule with a semicircular alcove on the back wall, faced with yellow Numidian marble. The helicoidal gallery which rises ten meters and leads to the funeral chamber begins to the right of the vestibule. The vault of this corridor, with four vertical light wells, is in rubblework; the pavement still retains traces of its original mosaic decoration while the walls were covered with marble to a height of three meters. The funeral chamber, right at the center of the massive drum, is square (3 m. per side) with three rectangular niches; illumination is from two oblique windows in the vault. The cinerary urns of the emperors were placed in this room. Above the funerary chamber were two superposed cellae which by means of an annular corridor led to the top of the monument.

As early as A.D. 403 the emperor Honorius may have incorporated the building in an outpost bastion of the Aurelian walls. In 537, when it was already a fortress, it was attacked by Vitiges and his Goths. In the 10th century it was transformed into a castle. Its appearance today is that of a massive fortress on a square base and with circular **towers** at the four corners (known as the towers of **St. Matthew, St. John, St. Mark,** and **St. Luke**) onto which a circular body has been grafted. This was built following the lines of the Imperial mausoleum under Benedict IX. Further work was ordered by Alexander VI and by Julius II who had the south loggia above the papal apartments added.

At the summit is the panoramic terrace, watched over by the *Angel* about to fly off, which seems to be why the building is called as it is, for the winged messenger is said to have saved Rome from a terrible plague at the time of Gregory the Great.

Inside the castle-fortress are the rooms of the **Museo Nazionale Militare** and of **Art**.

Right: Ponte Sant'Angelo and, below, the reconstruction of the Mausoleum of Hadrian on which Castel Sant'Angelo was built.

TRITON FOUNTAIN

Still another fascinating famous fountain by Gian Lorenzo Bernini is set in the center of the Piazza Barberini. Dating to 1643 it is characterized by the apparent lack of any kind of architectural support for the statue of the *Triton* from which the fountain takes its name. He is supported by a scallop shell which in turn rests on the arched tails of four dolphins. The water, which endows the whole ensemble with life, is naturalistically blown upwards by the Triton through a conch.

VIA VENETO

An important element in the town-planning projects of Rome at the beginning of the 20th century and the building up of the Ludovisi District, the Via Vittorio Veneto goes from the Piazza Barberini to the Porta Pinciana and is lined with outstanding works of architecture as well as with hotels, shops and universally famous rendezvous. Various periods of history are represented: the **Fountain of the Alps** by Bernini, the **Church of Santa Maria della Concezione** by Antonio Casoni, the **Church of Sant'Isidoro** (all 17th cent.) to the 20th-century **palaces** of the **Ministry of Industry and Trade** by Marcello Piacentini and Giuseppe Vaccaro, and the **Banca Nazionale del Lavoro**, also by Piacentini, as well as the **Palazzo Boncompagni-Ludovisi**, then **Margherita**, a late 19th-century work signed by Gaetano Koch.

Above, Piazza di Spagna seen from Trinità dei Monti and, below, the Fontana della Barcaccia by Pietro Bernini.

◄ Above: the Fontana del Tritone.
Below: the famous Via Veneto.

Above: the Casino Borghese. Below: the small Temple of Aesculapius in the park of Villa Borghese.

VILLA BORGHESE

First created for Cardinal Caffarelli Borghese early in the 17th century, the park was completely renewed at the end of the 18th century by the architects Asprucci and the painter Unterberger, but what we see now was the work of Luigi Canina at the beginning of the 19th century.

Generously donated to the city of Rome in 1902 by Umberto I, King of Italy, it was supposed to have been called after him. However, notwithstanding official names, it is still known as Villa Borghese in honor of the man who founded it.

This is the largest park in Rome with a perimeter of six kilometers and it is also the loveliest with a wealth of trees and charming paths. Entrance is from the overpass of the Viale dell'Obelisco, but also from the Porta Pinciana, Piazzale Flaminio and other minor entrances.

Above: the Gallery of the Emperors in the Museo Borghese.
Right: the bust of Cardinal Scipione Borghese by Bernini.

MUSEO AND GALLERIA BORGHESE

One of the most prestigious collections of sculpture and painting in the world is housed in the fine building known as the Casino Borghese, built for Cardinal Scipione Borghese by Giovanni Vasanzio (1613-1615). The Museum is installed on the ground floor and the itinerary leads through a portico, the Salone, and eight rooms, with various masterpieces by Bernini and Canova as well as examples of marble sculpture from Roman times. The Gallery, installed on the upper floor, has a spacious vestibule and twelve rooms and a selection of paintings which are truly priceless. A brief survey of the two famous collections follows.

Museo Borghese: Portico: sculpture from the Roman period and two panels of sarcophagi which depict the Muses.

Salone: twelve *busts* in colored marble by G. B. Della Porta (16th cent.) are in the niches; the vaults were frescoed by Mariano Rossi in the second half of the 18th century (*Camillus breaking off negotiations with Brennus* and the *Allegory of Glory*); the pavement contains five fragments of third-century mosaics (scenes of gladiators and the hunt). From the left, various pieces of antique sculpture (*Isis*, the *Satyr*, *Augustus*, a *Faun*, *Hadrian*, *Bacchus*, *Antoninus Pius*);

Room I (Sala della Paolina): the decoration on the vault

161

and walls (*Judgement of Paris* and *Stories of Aeneas*) by D. De Angelis; the highlight at the center of the room is *Paolina Borghese as Venus Victrix (1805)* by Canova, strikingly beautiful in its softly modeled forms and dominated by a subtle tempting sensuousness. *Room II* (of David): the frescoes in the vault are by Caccianiga (*Fall of Phaethon*); the five niches in the room contain five late Roman *busts*; but what most strikes the eye is the dynamic sculpture of *David*, an early work by Gian Lorenzo Bernini (1623-1624), at the center of the room. Around it are various Roman *statues*. **Room III** (of Apollo and Daphne). The fresco in the vault depicts the *Death of Daphne* by Pietro Angeletti. At the center is Bernini's wonderful sculpture of *Apollo and Daphne*, a bold and innovative work of 1624; the surrounding statues are Roman. **Chapel**: the walls are lined with *frescoes* by Deruet and Lanfranco; particularly noteworthy is a *female head with serpents* dating to the 5th century B.C. **Emperors' Gallery** (Room IV) with eighteen *Busts of Emperors* in porphyry and alabaster (17th cent.). The *Story of Galathea* is represented in the vault, at the center is the *Rape of Proserpine*, another example of Bernini's complex sculpture (1622); of particular note otherwise are the statues of *Dionysius* and the *Marine Venus*.

Room V (of the Hermaphrodite): in the vault *Hermaphrodite and Salmace* by Buonvicini; the Roman mosaic in the pavement has fishing scenes; of note the statue of the *Sleeping Hermaphrodite*, a reproduction of a Hellenistic original. **Room VI** (of Aeneas and Anchises): in the vault: the *Council of the Gods*, by Pacheux; at the center the marble group of *Aeneas and Anchises* by Gian Lorenzo and Pietro Bernini. The most striking piece on one side, among other Roman works, is *Truth unveiled by Time*, another important work by Bernini (1652). **Room VII** (Egyptian room): in the vault *frescoes* by T. Conca, in the pavement three Roman *mosaics*; the most striking of the other Roman statues is the *Youth on a Dolphin*, a copy of a Hellenistic original. **Room VIII** (of the Dancing Faun): in the vault, the *Sacrifice to Silenus* by T. Conca and, at the center, the *Dancing Faun*, a Roman copy of a Hellenistic original.

Galleria Borghese: **Vestibule**: housed here are the *Three Ages of Man*, painted by Sassoferrato, as well as works by Luca Cambiaso and Rutilio Manetti. **Room IX**: in the vault the *Stories of Aeneas* by A. De Maron (1786), particularly of note among the other works are the *Deposition*, one of Raphael's Roman masterpieces; the *Portrait of a Man* and the *Portrait of a Lady with a*

◄ The Rape of Proserpine (on the left) and Apollo and Daphne by Bernini (on the right).

Above: Paolina Borghese by Canova and, below, Bernini's David.

Unicorn, also by Raphael; the crystalline *Madonna and Child*, the *young Saint John and Angels* by Botticelli; the imposing *Holy Family* by Fra Bartolomeo, Perugino's *Madonna* and other works by Andrea del Sarto, Lorenzo di Credi, Santi di Tito, Mariotto Albertinelli, Pinturicchio. **Room X**: striking are the *Madonna and Child with the young St. John* by Andrea del Sarto, and Bronzino's dramatic *St. John the Baptist*; also works by Luca Cranach, Berruguete, Sodoma and Rosso Fiorentino. **Room XI**, with Lorenzo Lotto's *Madonna and Child with Saints* and his *Self-portrait*; of particular note, as well as works by Savoldo, Palma il Vecchio, and Bernini. **Room XII**: contains works by Annibale Carracci, Domenichino, Pietro da Cortona. **Room XIII**: contains works by Giulio Romano, Puligo, Scipione Pulzone, Franciabigio. **Room XIV**: in the vault the *Council of the Gods* by Lanfranco. Particular mention among the works exhibited goes to the *David with the head of Goliath*, the *Madonna of the Serpent* (painted for the Palafrenieri), and *St. John the Baptist in the Desert*, three sublime paintings by Caravaggio; there are also works by A. Carracci, Guercino, and some realistic sculpture by Bernini. **Room XV**: in the vault, *Allegory of Aurora* by D. Corvi. **Room XVI**: in the ceiling, *Flora* by G. B. Marchetti; the room is almost completely

Above, left: Boy with Basket of Fruit by Caravaggio; right: Botticelli's tondo of the Madonna and Child with the Infant St. John and Saints. Below: Sacra Conversazione by Lorenzo Lotto.

dedicated to the works of Iacopo Bassano. **Room XVII**: in the vault, *Story of Walter of Angers* by G. Cades; as well as works by Dossi, Garofalo, Scarsellino, Francia. **Room XVIII**: in the vault, *Jupiter and Antiope* by B. Gagneraux; outstanding are many paintings by Rubens, his famous

Susanna and the Elders and the *Deposed Christ* and some paintings by Mandekens, Brill, Sustris, and other Flemish artists. **Room XIX**: among the many works exhibited in this room mention must be made of Correggio's touching and intimate **Danaë** and various paintings by Dossi, Pordenone, Parmigianino. **Room XX**: here are some of Titian's masterpieces, such as *Sacred and Profane Love*, *Venus Blindfolding Cupid*, and *St. Domenic*; Antonello da Messina's profoundly introspective *Portrait of a Man* and works by Veronese, Bellini and Carpaccio.

Portrait of a Young Man by Ghirlandaio.

Preaching of the Baptist by Veronese.

The Holy Family by Sodoma.

Portrait of a Courtesan by Carpaccio.

PIAZZA DI SPAGNA AND TRINITÀ DEI MONTI

One of the most characteristic squares in the city, the Piazza di Spagna, stretches out for over 270 meters, divided into two triangular areas. It is surrounded by outstanding buildings, such as the **Palazzo di Propaganda Fide**, seat of the *Congregation of Propaganda Fide* instituted by Pope Gregory XV in 1622. The facade on the square is by Bernini (1644) and is articulated in three floors. The sober, elegant design is in brick. The more complex facade at the side however is by Borromini (1665) and is concave in the center. It is articulated by pilaster strips which reach up to the first floor where unique concave windows are set off by columns and pilasters. The large portal leads to the vestibule with, nearby, Borromini's **Church of the Magi** (dei Re Magi) (1666). The restrained luminous interior has a fine *Adoration of the Magi* by Giacinto Gemignani (1643). Another noteworthy complex is the **Palazzo di Spagna** built by A. Del Grande in 1647 which has an important facade with lovely portals tied together by severe rustication. The square is centered on the **Barcaccia Fountain**, by Pietro Bernini (1627-1629), an ingenious and lively representation of a large boat which is sinking and spouting water from both stern and prow. Piazza di Spagna is where the famous **Spanish Steps (Scalinata di Trinità dei Monti)** begin. Built entirely in travertine by Francesco De Sanctis (1723-1726) the twelve flights of steps of varying widths branch off into various blocks as they move upward towards the Piazza Trinità dei Monti. At the center of the square is the *Sallustian Obelisk* which comes from the Sallustian Gardens. The square is dominated by the powerful structures of the **Church of Trinità dei Monti**, one of the most imposing Franciscan churches in the city. Begun in 1503 at the request of Louis XII, the church has been remodelled at various times. The sober facade, by Carlo Maderno, with a single order of pilasters and a broad portal with columns and a large balustrade, is preceded by a staircase by Domenico Fontana that is decorated with capitals and antique bas-reliefs. The interior has a single large nave and contains fine works of art including a lovely fresco with *Stories of St. John the Baptist* by Naldini, in the first chapel on the right; Daniele da Volterra's famous and brilliant *Assumption*, in the third chapel on the right. The second chapel on the left contains the *Deposition*, another masterpiece by Daniele da Volterra, and in the sixth chapel on the left, Perin del Vaga's *Assumption* and *Isaiah and Daniel* (on the front of the tomb), Taddeo Zuccari's *Death of Maria* and the *Assumption* by Federico and Taddeo Zuccari. Another outstanding work by Federico Zuccari, the *Coronation of the Virgin*, is in the chapel to the left of the presbytery. The **Cloister** contains frescoes by various artists with *Stories from the life of Saint Francis of Paola*.

The Spanish Steps leading to Trinità dei Monti from Piazza di Spagna.

◄ Piazza Navona with the Neptune Fountain and the Church of Sant'Agnese in Agone.

Fontana dei Fiumi (Fountain of the Four Rivers) by Bernini in the center of Piazza Navona.

PIAZZA NAVONA

The most famous square of Baroque Rome stands on the site of Domitian's stadium and the name seems to derive from a popular corruption of the term for the competitive games « *in agone* » which were held here. From the times of Domitian on, the place was used almost exclusively for sports events, including the famous August regatta in which the participants wore the colors of the nobles and the civic clergy. Even now the feast of the *Befana* (the Italian version of Santa Claus who arrives on January 6th) is celebrated

there in January with a typical market. But the real attraction of the square is the famous **Fountain of the Four Rivers** by Gian Lorenzo Bernini, dated 1651, and thanks to which the artist gained the admiration and protection of the pope then in office, Innocent X. The rivers represented in the fountain are the Danube, the Ganges, the Nile, the Rio de la Plata. They are arranged on a steep rocky reef from which a Roman obelisk taken from the Circus of Maxentius daringly rises up into the air. In line with the Fountain of the Four Rivers are the **Fountain of the Moor**, in front of the **Palazzo Pamphili**, and the **Fountain of Neptune**, formerly of the *Calderari*, at the northern end of the square.

APPIA ANTICA AND TOMB OF CAECILIA METELLA

The most important of the Roman consular roads, known as *Regina Viarum* (the queen of roads), begins at Porta San Sebastiano and winds towards the interior bordered with ancient monuments and others that are not so old. Miraculous events such as the famous « *Domine quo vadis?* » are thought to have taken place here.

The **Tomb of Caecilia Metella** lies on the Via Appia Antica. This sumptuous mausoleum, a typical example, was originally built for Caecilia, wife of Crassus and daughter of Quintus Metellus, conqueror of Crete. It belongs to the late republican period and was modified in 1302 by the Caetani who adapted it as a tower to defend their neighboring castle. Even so the tomb chamber of the ancient tomb with its conical cover can still be identified.

CATACOMBS

These deep galleries were once quarries for travertine and pozzolana. Situated at the periphery of Rome, they became meeting places for the early Christians and shortly thereafter were also used as cemeteries (1st-4th cent.). Mention will be made of those of Domitilla, Saint Calixtus, Saint Sebastian, Saint Agnes and Priscilla. In the 16th century they were rediscovered and reappraised after centuries of abandon.

The **Catacombs of Saint Domitilla**, known also as catacombs of SS. Achilleus and Nereus, are the largest in Rome and traditionally developed from a simple family burial ground that belonged to Domitilla, wife or niece of the consul Flavius Clemente put to death by Domitian. The catacombs contain the remains of the Basilica of SS. Nereus and Achilleus, behind the apse of which is a cubicle with the fresco of the *Deceased Veneranda invoking St. Petronilla*. The ancient burial grounds of the Aurelian Flavians lie near the basilica. In another part of the catacombs, named after the *Good Shepherd* because the earliest representation of this subject was found here, paintings from the 2nd century are to be found in the vault. Lastly, in the area of later date there are fine depictions of the grain market, scenes of daily life and work (3rd-4th cent.).

The **Catacombs of Saint Calixtus** are just as famous and extend for twenty kilometers. They were developed by Pope Calixtus III and became the official burial grounds for the bishops of Rome. They are excavated on four levels and contain the *Crypt of the Popes*, in which several of the early popes were buried. They contain interesting decorations as well as epigraphs of Pontianus Lucius Eutychianus and Sixtus II. The *Cubiculum of Saint Cecilia*, where the remains of this Christian martyr were found, is decorated with painting from the 7th and and 8th centuries. After this comes the *Gallery of the Sepulchers*, again with interesting paintings, the fine *Crypt of Pope Eusebius* and the *Crypt of Lucina*. The most remote parts of the necropolis (2nd cent. A.D.) are decorated with paintings of fish and symbols of the Eucharist.

The **Catacombs of Saint Sebastian** are also excavated on four levels: the first has been partially destroyed but still has an austere chapel where St. Philip Neri used to go to pray; on the second floor is an intimate crypt, known as the *Crypt of Saint Sebastian*, with a *Bust of the saint* attributed to Bernini. An underground passage leads to three tombs with decorations and stuccoes dating to the 1st century A.D.

◄ The Tomb of Caecilia Metella on the Via Appia Antica.

The statue of St. Sebastian in the Basilica of San Sebastiano.

The votive statue of St. Cecilia in the Catacombs of St. Calixtus.

IN MEMORY OF EDITH CECILIA McBRIDE OF NEW YORK U.S.A.

Above: the Palazzo della Civiltà del Lavoro and, below, the Palazzo dell'ENI, in the EUR.

E.U.R.

This famous district, at one and the same time the most recent and the most historical, was originally created for the Esposizione Universale di Roma (World Fair of Rome) to be held in 1942. Designed by a group of famous architects (Pagano, Piccinato, Vietti, and Rossi) coordinated and directed by Marcello Piacentini, it covers an area of 420 hectares in the shape of a pentagon.

The formative concept was that of monumentality and it was built with a view to the future expansion of Rome towards the Tyrrhenian Sea. Included among its significant paradigms of Italian architecture of the first half of the 20th century are the **Palazzo della Civiltà del Lavoro**, as well as the sites of the **Museo Preistorico ed Etnografico Pigorini**, the **Museo dell'Alto Medioevo (Early Middle Ages)**, the **Museo delle Arti e Tradizioni Popolari** and the **Museo della Civiltà Romana**.

Tivoli: Villa d'Este.

TIVOLI

...LA D'ESTE

...outside Rome, Tivoli, the ancient *Tibur*, was already ...ite holiday resort for the Romans as well as a place ...worship of local divinities. It is now the site of the ...egoriana, a fine **Cathedral**, the renowned **Rocca** ...above all, the **Villa d'Este**, with an Italian garden ...ly famous for its magic atmosphere.

...he ruins of a Roman villa, it was first a Benedictine ...and then the Governor's Palace, and as such was ...ently restored by Pirro Ligorio on commission of ...rnor at the time, Ippolito d'Este, around 1550. Af-...us vicissitudes it became the property of Austria, ...urned to the Italians in 1918, then restored before ...nnumental part and the immense park were opened ...public. Of note on the grounds is the **Loggia** by Pirro ...io, which is the finest part of the main facade which ...s the city and the mountains.

...e **Italian gardens**, with their geometric compartmen-...lization, the fiwaterve hundred fountains, the age and rar-ity of the trees, is certainly one of the finest gardens to be found both in and outside Italy. No visit is complete without a stop at the *Grotto of Diana*, richly stuccoed with mythological scenes, the so-called « *Rometta* » or little Rome, with reproductions in an allusive key of parts of the city (the Isola Tiberina, the ruins), the various *Fountains of*

Bacchus, the *Organ Fountain* (the water organ was designed by Claudio Vernard), the *fountains of Proserpine, of the Dragons* (signed by Ligorio), *of the « Mete », of the Eagles*, and so on, up to the romantic *Cypress Rotonda*. Even in this end of the garden signs of antiquity are present, as witnessed by the ruins of a **Roman villa** to the right of the Cypress Rotonda.

HADRIAN'S VILLA

Tivoli is also the site of an imposing architectural complex dating to Hadrian's time. This emperor's gifts as an architect can be seen in the series of palaces, baths, theaters, etc. which he had built there between 118 and 134, and which were meant to remind him, here in Italy, of the places he most loved in Greece and the Near East.

Mentioned for the first time in literature by Flavio Biondo, the Villa, or rather what was left of it, was visited and studied by famous persons (Pope Pius II, Pirro Ligorio) and excavations were carried out particularly in the 18th century (Piranesi made engravings of some parts). Bought by the Italian government in 1870 from the Braschi family which had owned it since the beginning of the 19th century, the villa was restored, while many of the works of art (especially sculpture) from the site can now be seen in the rooms of the Museo Nazionale Romano.

CONTENTS